Quiet Time

Vol. 1

Quiet Time

Vol. 1

From My

"Quiet Time"

To Yours

A Book of Inspired Poetry and Psalms

by
Gary Rutter

Copyright © 2015 by Gary Rutter, Author

Reach The World Publishing
PO Box 262
Hyde, PA 16843
www.garybaileyministries.com

First Printing, June, 2016
Printed in the United States of America

All rights reserved under International Copyright Law. Reproduction of text or cover in whole or in part without the express written consent by the author is not permitted and is unlawful according to the 1976 United States Copyright Act.

Foreword by Rev. Gary Bailey

Quiet Time: (Vol. 1) From My Quiet Time To Yours- A Book of Inspired Poetry and Psalms
ISBN- 1-943256-03-9
ISBN- 978-1-943256-03-7

Unless otherwise indicated, all Scripture quotations are taken from the **King James Version** of the Bible.

Reach The World Publishing

Dedication

To God my Father who has become intimately involved in my life, communes with me in the person of The Holy Spirit, He puts His arm around me and guides me through the stuff. To Jesus Christ, my Lord, my Brother, my Friend, who was obedient in taking the suffering and death that was due me and rose again victoriously and freely shares His victory with me. Eternity won't be long enough to say: "Thank You Jesus". To The Holy Spirit my constant Companion, my Confidant, my Life Source and Inspiration. To God be the Glory, Great things He has done!

Table of Contents

Dedication
Table of Contents
Foreword
Preface
Acknowledgements
Introduction

December 30, 2014..1
(Personal Prophecy for Donna)

January 11, 2015 3
Keep Yourself Free

January 14, 2015... 5
Stir Up the Gift

January 20, 2015 6
Personal Prophecy for Myself

January 21, 2015... 8
Personal Prophecy for Myself

January 23, 2015. 10
We're in A War, Learn to Fight

January 25, 2015 12
Your Life Is Lost

January 26, 2015 13
The Time Has Come

January 27, 2015..15
You'll Know My Way, Look for The Sign

January 28, 2015. 16
Of My Spirit Just for You

February 1, 2015. 18
To Them We Speak a Mystery

February 2, 2015.. 20
This Life I Have Deep Inside

February 4, 2015... 22
  "You Will Have No 'Word' If You Can See No Good."

February 5, 2015 23
  How Does That Work?

February 6, 2015.. 25
  A Song and Dance Will Not Do

February 9, 2015.. 28
  Concerning A Vision

February 10, 2015 29
  When You Lift Up a Shout

February 11, 2015.. 30
  The Lord Will Keep the Feet of His Saints

February 16, 2015 32
  Leave This World a Better Place

February 23, 2015... 33
  To My Father Gladly I Ran

February 24, 2015... 36
  What Is It That You Do?

February 25, 2015... 38
  The Last Call Is Sounding Now!

February 26, 2015... 39
  You've Been Slow in The Past

February 28, 2015..41
  Out of My Heart

March 2, 2015 43
  I Won't Sit Here While Life Goes By

March 4, 2015 46
  Human History

March 9, 2015 47
  Your Life Has Only Been Lent

March 18, 2015 49
  Some Are Red, Some Are Blue

March 19, 2015 52
  I See You Lord, And That's Enough

March 20, 2015 53
  Just Another Day, But Yet

March 26, 2015 54
  I'll Love Him Too, In Jesus Name

March 27, 2015 55
  Because You Dared To Follow Me

April 4, 2015 56
  If In My Plan You Want A Part

April 7, 2015 58
  So Lord, My God, And My Friend

April 9, 2015 60
  Just One Voice

April 10, 2015 62
  I Want You to Live Innocently

April 11, 2015 63
  I Was Just A Kid In Those Days

April 23, 2015 64
  This Open Door Will Soon Close

April 24, 2015 66
  What Is True Is What Endures

April 27, 2015 66
  But Wait God

April 28, 2015 69
  Jesus Is The Standard

May 4, 2015 70
  With The Blood I Agree

May 5, 2015 72
  One Way

May 13, 2015 73
  You Can't Fake It

May 14, 2015 74
    Appointed to This Very Hour

May 19, 2015 76
    Do What He Says

May 21, 2015 79
    No Lofty Perch

May 25, 2015 80
    Your Need Is Great

May 27, 2015 81
    Love of The Father

June 1, 2015 82
    Move On

June 3, 2015 82
    We Can Keep It

June 8, 2015 83
    This Is What I Pray for You

June 15, 2015 84
    The Cross

June 16, 2015 86
    The Bottom Rung

June 19, 2015 89
    The Night Is Far Spent

June 22, 2015 90
    Get Rid of the Cow

June 23, 2015 93
    Out of The Blue

June 24, 2015 94
    There Is No End

June 26, 2015 96
    Many Mysteries

July 6, 2015 97
    On Wings of Eagles

July 7, 2015 98
   Show Me How

July 13, 2015 101
   God Never Changes

July 15, 2015 101
   Thank You Lord

July 21, 2015 102
   Through A Hole

July 22, 2015... 104
   The Love of The Father

July 30, 2015...105
   And Then Some Day

July 31, 2015 107
   The Curse Causeless

August 3, 2015 108
   Only Believe

August 5, 2015 110
   I Guess Not

August 5, 2015 110
   Take Your Rest

August 7, 2015 111
   I Am The Way

August 8, 2015 113
   Haroon and Maddie

August 11, 2015 114
   To The Point

August 14, 2015... 115
   Do It Now

August 18, 2015 117
   The Prettiest Thing You've Ever Seen

August 24, 2015 118
   Moving On

August 26, 2015 119
   That Sacred Desk

August 27, 2015 121
   If I Seem to Lack

August 31, 2015..122
   But for Now

September 5, 2015 122
   The War

September 8, 2015..124
   All Is Well

September 10, 2015 126
   Make Us Preachers

September 12, 2015 128
   The Unseen Trade

September 14, 2015 129
   Hidden Treasure

September 16, 2015 130
   The Sower Soweth

September 21, 2015 131
   Prophets, Wise Men, and Scribes

September 23, 2015..133
   Yesterday's Manna

September 25, 2015 135
   Then Jesus Came

September 29, 2015...137
   It Is with You as Was Foretold

October 2, 2015..138
   Look for Good

October 7, 2015...139
   Great Reward

October 8, 2015 140
   This Is The Day

October 9, 2015 143
   Break The Mold

October 16, 2015 145
   Good News for Everyone

October 19, 2015 147
   First Frost

October 26, 2015 147
   Singing His Song

November 4, 2015 149
   Dogs Bark

November 11, 2015 150
   The Unseen

November 13, 2015 152
   As a Child

November 17, 2015 153
   Prophesy

November 19, 2015 155
   The Upper Room

December 1, 2015 156
   His Message I Will Always Be

December 4, 2015 158
   The Time at Hand

December 14, 2015 159
   But for Grace

December 22, 2015 161
   A Blooming Flower Will Be Found

   Scripture References 163

Foreword

Gary Rutter is a man of prayer and few words. When he does speak, I have learned to listen because it is sure to be significant and something to be remembered. The psalmist speaks of a deep call:

<u>Deep calleth unto deep at the noise of thy waterspouts: all thy waves and thy billows are gone over me (Psalm 42:7)</u>

The meditations of a man's heart are cultivated in that secret place with God. As a man seeks the Kingdom of God and searches the depths of his heart and soul, treasures from heaven are uncovered that otherwise would remain buried. I know that in the following pages are great treasures of grace and truth that will draw you into a deeper place in God. These passages are of such spiritual quality that you will want to read them again and again. These musings of the heart will leave you with the stamp of heaven on your soul and the light of God in your eyes. This book of poetry is a flowing river that cascades from the author's innermost being. As you read and meditate upon the pages in this book, you will sense the nearness of God and experience that deep place from which these writings have come.

Brother Gary Bailey
May 19th, 2016

Preface

I began an early morning prayer habit and was careful to journal, date, time and any notes that might come to me that day. These usually would have to do with what I preach or teach at church, but not always. Eventually I found that writing poetry was a way to draw from my spirit. Over the course of a year, 2015 I ended with a book of poems.
(re: poem from Jan 21)

Acknowledgements

God, it seems, has used nearly everybody to speak into my life, even pets and nature itself (Rom 1:20). I have had so many profound teachers, all of whom I am most grateful to have had the privilege to learn from.

Rev. Rob Laero is a name I will mention, he is my friend and brother in The Lord. He has a passion for prayer and kept after me about having a prayer meeting. Just what I didn't want, another meeting. I finally gave in. On Sunday evenings we meet at the Church to pray. Over the years the opportunity to pray in the morning came up so I pray then as well. It was while Rob and I were praying on a Sunday evening that God said to me "write".

Rev. Gary Bailey, of course, I must acknowledge my good friend and Brother in The Lord. Gary was our very first Itinerate Preacher at our Church and we've been great friends ever since. He is always an encourager. He is excited about this book and offered to put it together for me. So of course I agreed. It is of indispensable importance to have someone who believes in you! Thank you Gary and Gwen.

Of course my wife Catherine, the one who knows me the best and loves me the most, is definitely a miracle. She is my wife of 49 years. We were just kids starting out, and we didn't know anything, but God had a plan. She and my wonderful family tolerate me and all my shortcomings, most of the time. They can be found in the poem from February 28.

Introduction

It was in the habit of prayer, nearly every Sunday evening at the Church with Brother Rob Laero that I regularly noted in my journal whatever The Lord seemed to say to me. On one such occasion The Lord said "write", so I wrote in my journal "write". Some weeks later for the third time God said "write", which I did and I added in my journal, "what"? I was truly perplexed as to what The Lord wanted me to write. About the same time a dear friend of our Church lost her father. We found out after the fact and missed the memorial service. We didn't send a card or flowers. So my wife and I decided to send a card with a check in it. Before we sent it, I was in prayer and these words came, "The money will go and the flowers will fade," I knew God was talking so I went to my journal and wrote it down, and just kept writing and writing. Sometimes I couldn't write fast enough. I completed the poem, typed it and sent it with the card to our friend. With her permission, I have included this first poem in my book. I am confident that many will find comfort in this poem because The Lord is in it. Through 2015, The Lord has continued to bless me with over 100 inspired poems. Some of them will bless you more than others. My favorite is February 28. Two of them changed my ministry, January 20 and 21.

There is something for just about everybody, even a couple for my atheist friends, for God truly loves us all and would not that any should perish.

Only Believe.

<u>December 30, 2014</u>

(Personal Prophecy for Donna)

The money will go; the flowers will fade.
Fond memories of Dad, are like afternoon shade.
A place I can go, to get away from the heat,
Though it's all in my mind, the relief is so sweet.

I know he likes heaven, and will not return,
But I will see him again, and for now I must learn,
That my life here is almost complete,
And soon I will join him, at Jesus feet.

To love and be loved, as never before,
There with my Dad, forevermore.
With these kind thoughts, I now go my way,
And listen for Jesus, to guide me each day.

Thank you Jesus, for touching my heart.
I'm happy for Dad, though for now we're apart.
As a pilgrim I go, this world isn't home.
I'll take comfort in knowing, I am never alone.

For Jesus is with me, each step of the way,
And that great cloud of witnesses, is there every day.
To cheer me along, when Jesus I hear,
And do as he said with no need to fear.

Dad's life here with me, has come to a close,
But my love for him, continues to grow.
For each day that passes, I see in him more,
The God given gift, and now I am sure.

That God in His wisdom, was speaking to me,
Through the life of my Dad, though I could not see.
But now I will savor, as the future unfolds,
The things that I missed, that plainly he told.

If only I'd known, the gift that God gave,
God and my Dad, both wanted me saved.
Thanks again Lord, for letting me see,
How you through my Dad, have always loved me.

In that great cloud of witnesses, my Dad has his part.
So I now run my race, with all of my heart.
He never has tears, by what he can see,
For there is only joy, when He's looking at me.

If I make Heaven happy, They'll see me often,
So I'll set my course, to not be forgotten.
My Dad will be happy, and Jesus too,
When they see all the kindness, that I can do.

For I am not helpless, nor hopeless at all.
Jesus is with me, even when I fall.
His mercy unfailing, His love tried and true,
Jesus has always, for me come through.

So Jesus I ask you, as we travel on,
Tell Dad I miss him, although he's not gone.
With You he takes joy, each time that he sees
Your will accomplished, even in me.

So I too am happy, as onward I go,
For I will follow Jesus, and my Dad will know.

Pastor Gary Rutter

January 11, 2015

Keep Yourself Free

There will be those who come
With their minds made up
Of what they want to see,
But they have not known my ways
And they will reject thee.

Still more will come not knowing
What to expect from you.
When they get here they will see
That it's not you but I that move.

The blind will see,
The lame will walk,
The deaf will hear,
And the dumb will talk.

Though My flame will burn bright
Keep this prayer time dear,
For though the miracles are sight
It's this prayer time that you'll hear.

As I lead you in prayer,
Be faithful to do.
I'll meet with you there,
And in the works you do too.

Over and over My plan is for you
To move as I beckon and you will prove,
My faithfulness is sure I will not fail,
And on the wings of eagles my people will sail.

As I call on you and lead you higher and higher,
My Church will consume chaff with Holy Ghost Fire,
Until My Bride is ready for that day,
When I shall come and catch her away.

Listen, listen and pray,
For this is surely the day,
When My Word goes forth
And My Church rises, a mighty force.

Plundering hell and populating Heaven,
In the gifts and callings that I have given.
Soon, very soon if you follow you'll see,
My Power and Glory, yes even Me.

For I shall appear in the clouds on high,
And it won't be long till I'm seen in the sky.
So this is the time don't hesitate
To do my will before it's too late.

My plans for you will soon come to be,
And as you Preach and Pray others will see,
That I stand by My Word I'm always true,
And they shall be free, and on fire too.

For this is the day when My Church will shine,
And bring in the Great Harvest, for now it is time.
By My Spirit, My power, My Church will grow,
Because it is time and this you should know.

Keep yourself free
And listen to Me,
My love for you
Will always shine through

Others will Know
And they'll want to go,
With you to the harvest,
For they will be blessed.

January 14, 2015

Stir Up the Gift

Stir up the gift in your heart,
For in God's great choir you have a part,
To sing and fill the air with sound,
The music of Heaven here to abound.

That every ear,
Be blessed to hear,
About the One,
Who holds us dear.

For Jesus is the One we love,
And why not with Heavens Dove,
Lift Him up for all to see,
Why with our heart we are so free.

Sing, sing then, and Praise the Lord,
And when you are done, sing some more,
The song of the redeemed forevermore,
So The Lamb who was slain will have His reward.

As we sing Jesus praise,
Through all of our days,
The world will catch on,
To Heavens beautiful song.

Soon the tune with message clear,
Will be sung by so many, all will hear.
How Jesus loves them, more than they know.
They too will change, and to Jesus go.

To get a song for their heart,
And in God's choir take their part.
To sing and praise,
And worship always.

Until all of Heaven, and earth be filled,
With the praise of God, our hearts to thrill.
At the wonder of all the love that can be,
In a heart filled with praise, so full and free.

If with these lines you now are bored,
Stir up the gift, and Praise the Lord!

January 20, 2015
Personal Prophecy for Myself

The pudding is not eaten; many have not returned.
They don't bring their friends, so the lesson is learned.
Except the Lord build the house, they labor in vain,
and the forty empty chairs, witness a message of pain.

You're on the wrong road, they sit there and shout.
Their witness is clear, and so follows doubt.
Did I not hear? Did I not listen?
Have I chosen my way, and not the Word that was given?

Forty witnesses have spoken, loud and clear.
Your vision is broken; now will you hear?
It's almost too late, no time to wait,
your call is to write, better get it right.

The forty don't lie, they have a reason.
They're not coming, They're not tease'n.
They don't see the gift, that God has given.
It's not in the speaking, it must be written.

Get on with it now, don't labor in vain.
You've built your own house; it's causing you pain.
They don't bring their friends, the pudding's not fit.
The Gift is not seen, the chairs empty sit.

The Gift is within, dig down deep.
My Word is written, a promise to keep.
To have and to hold, not fleeting away,
Take it and read it, any time, any day.

It's important to write, people tend to forget.
What they heard may be right, but to read better yet.
My Word has been written, for this very reason.
You can have it always, not just for a season.

If you write it in rhyme, it will be read out loud.
Then time after time, the message goes out.
It's not just something someone had to say.
Here for the moment, then fleeting away.

Put it in writing. It will keep on fighting,
To get their attention, and did I mention?
For this very reason, I have recorded,
My Word in the Bible, your steps are now ordered.

Blessings untold, wait for the writing.
Your future unfolds, My Spirit's inviting,
You to follow, as I build,
no more labor in vain, my house will be filled.

<u>January 21, 2015</u>

Personal Prophecy for Myself

Deep calls unto deep, from way down inside.
A yearning comes up, it will no longer hide.
A hunger from deep within,
stirring now, because of Him.

The Spirit of God, down in my heart,
It's time to awake, and do your part.
As I acknowledge, the stirring inside,
It only gets stronger, no place to hide.

I cannot deny, what's in my heart.
For it will not tarry, it drives me to start.
My pencil on paper, if I want to obey,
Then I will hear, what He has to say.

My people are yearning to hear from Me.
You keep on writing, then they will see.
I speak by My Spirit, to the hearts of men.
If at first they don't listen, I say it again.

You'll go no further, with Me in the lead,
Until you obey, what I said to thee.
Now keep on writing, for the longer you go,
The deeper you'll dig, My Word to know.

The secret of life, will always be,
Revealed to those, who listen to Me.
When you begin to write My Words down,
Then you will see, my direction you've found.

It is not hidden, or far from thee,
Deep in your heart, is where I speak.
You'll help yourself by listening to Me.
Then others too, will begin to see.

When I give you a Word for one you hold dear,
Then write it in rhyme and they will hear.
The secrets I've spoken, deep in their inside,
Are spoken to them by you in a rhyme.

My witness they'll hear and in their heart too.
My Spirit will say, "you know this is true.
I've gone a long way, to get it to you.
My servant has spoken and My Spirit has too".

Now take this Word, and be on your way.
Because you have listened, you start a new day.
With Me in the lead, you have a fresh start.
Be sure to remember, I'm deep in your heart.

Deep calls to deep,
I hope you will listen,
Then I know you will find,
What you have been miss'n.

January 23, 2015.

We're in A War, Learn to Fight

Now faith is the substance, of things hoped for
The evidence, of things unseen
When I speak the words you spoke to me Lord
It becomes a Holy Seed

When I say, what I don't see
It's heavens way, of blessing me
To walk by faith, and not by sight
It's Jesus way, His way is right

Without faith, He is not pleased
So I'll go on, sowing seed
When by faith, I call what's not
As though it were, my course I'll plot

Some believe when they see
But Jesus said: follow me
Walk by faith, not by sight
We're in a war, now learn to fight

Not in the flesh, as others do
but in the spirit, you must be true
What My Word says, is no lie
By faith you'll live, or else you'll die

Take My lead, learn to say
What you read, in My Word today
Call them well, who now are ill
Then by My Word I will heal

My Word is sown, when you speak
It will not come home incomplete
It will do just what I said
Speak from your heart and not your head

In My kingdom, faith is the rule
Move in the spirit where I will school
In the way that you must go
So start to say My Word follow

My Word is alive when you speak
By faith you'll fight, the mountain peak
While others climb, up to its top
You will remove it, from its spot

So say it now and do not doubt
Follow Me; learn to shout
The devils tremble when in My name
you disassemble their domain

The flesh is plainly in your face
But I've called you to run the race
When you speak what you believe
What is sight will take to flight

Mountains move when you say
My Word in you so start today
While My Spirit to you beckons
Do it now before you reckon

That this word is but a rhyme
Before its stolen this is the time
Of your decision Heaven's waiting
But for a moment no hesitating

From whence it comes no one knows
So My Spirit comes and goes
God's time is now please don't slack
Put your hand to the plow and don't look back

January 25, 2015
Your Life Is Lost

Take up your cross and follow Me
Your life is lost but you will see
If you follow Me I will lead
I'll make your life a Holy seed

I will sow where others go
But where that is you don't know
I'll plant you in the earth with man
My life will spring from desert sand

Where I plant you will flourish
Where others can't you will nourish
My people yearn to hear my voice
With you they'll learn it is their choice

To believe when they pray
In their heart hear what I say
Words and action must there be
Then My glory they will see

January 26, 2015

The Time Has Come

The time has come this is the hour
We'll know the strength of this world's power
Heaven's window is open and falling down
Comes tons of wealth to the ground

In this world where we live
God has purposed us to give
To His harvest these last days
But we must stick to God's ways

Why would He say to me,
Here's My money I'm trusting thee?
When I appeared to the eleven
I said you're in charge then went to heaven

They were just mortal men
I sent them to Jerusalem
Wait for power from on high
Then you'll see the reason why

I can trust you if you wait
On the Holy Ghost don't be late
With My Spirit you will see
Just how well you'll follow Me

I'll have My way before I'm done
To My harvest you will run
Souls to rescue souls to save
Precious souls in every place

You cannot do it by yourself.
There are many for you to help.
When they've wakened to the task
I'll have My harvest at long last.

Gifts and callings that I've given
Need a stirring toward the vision.
No excuse anymore,
Here's the cash there's the door.

I will ignite a fire in you.
It will burn in others too.
With My fire they will run
till all of My souls are won.

You must believe it to receive it.
If you are ready, you'll be steady.
If you're not, then your lot
will be sorrow if you don't follow.

I've kept you small for a reason.
There are times, there are seasons.
Few there are that I can trust
for the money not to lust.

The time has come, it's not too late.
Now on My Spirit you must wait.
You were not ready at all before.
Come in closer, and close the door.

I will impart to you a mystery.
There's just one time in all of history
For Me to do the thing at last,
That's not been done in the past.

From a single wave I will begin
a mighty flood, many souls to win.
By My Spirit, and My Word,
the greatest sound, you ever heard.

As a rushing mighty wind
I'll fill My house and all of them
who now sit waiting on Me
will suddenly jump to their feet.

And to the streets they will go
as they did long ago.
I'll turn this world upside down
just before the trumpet sounds.

In the sky I will appear
to catch away, those I hold dear.
Your time is come, your season is here.
Now I've made it very clear.

January 27, 2015.

You'll Know My Way, Look for The Sign

This is the day to look for Me.
If you look you will see.
My Word working everywhere
You will no longer have a care.

When you watch and follow Me
All your cares will start to flee.
One by one they'll be gone
Some at dusk some at dawn.

Light and lively you will be
When all your cares you give to Me.
I can use you if you're free
I have plans to complete.

You have a part in what I do
So don't lose heart follow through.
Now is the day, now is the time
You'll know My way look for the sign.

Peace and joy in the Holy Ghost
Righteousness is what you need most.
For there is no condemnation
When by My Spirit We are one.

As you travel through this day
Look for Me seek My way.
You will not be the same
Now go out in Jesus Name.

And be My witness in the earth
To many souls I'll give birth.
As you go you will know
I Am with you; My Word is so.

January 28, 2015.

Of My Spirit Just for You

There is a place where I abide
In your heart down deep inside.
If you want to hear from Me
You must learn to dig deep.

Turn off your head and instead
Learn to hear what is so near.
It is not far or hard to find
When you are at peace of mind.

Too many things demand attention
Heaven waits for your decision.
Will you trust them to the Lord?
Can you take Him at His Word?

If you can rest from those cares
You will escape the devil's snare.
No more bound to that dimension
I will have your full attention.

I will speak with you there
In that place that is where
I have made My abode
And you come without a load.

For your cares don't you see
Cannot come in with you and Me.
Us alone is where you'll find
I will impart peace of mind.

At the altar give up the cares
Before you enter this place in prayer.
The Holiest Place is in your heart
It is there I will impart.

Of My Spirit just for you
Direct from Me a Word of truth.
I will commune with you there
And lift you from the world of care.

Righteousness you will find
From My Spirit peace of mind.
And with joy you will go out
Where you go you'll want to shout.

"God's alive in My heart
For to me He did impart
Peace and joy deep inside
Now in Him I will abide"

Cast your care on Me today.
I care for you in every way.
Then to you I will impart
Peace and joy in your heart.

<u>February 1, 2015.</u>
To Them We Speak a Mystery
[1] (Based on 1Cor. Ch. 2)

All the excellent words, and wisdom declared,
Could not my heart bare.
Christ and Him crucified,
Was it for me He died?

Something from the Preacher came,
But not with enticing words, my heart changed.
'Twas The Spirit and Power that broke through,
And deep inside made my heart new.

My faith stands not on thought and reason,
Nor on vain philosophies of men.
The Power of God came into me,
And in my heart has set me free.

A Spirit message I now speak,
To them alive in Spirit receive.
Not of this world can understand,
With their ears hear only man.

To them we speak a mystery,
Hidden of God before history.
With their mind they could not see,
Or they would not have slain The Lord of Glory.

Eye hath not seen nor ear heard,
Nor entered the heart what God prepared.
We who love Him have received it,
He hath revealed it by His Spirit.

The Spirit searches the deep things
And to us imparts the blessing.
No one can know another's heart,
Only that other can impart,

The secrets held deep inside,
Where His Spirit does reside.
So with God no one can know,
Lest by His Spirit He does show.

Now His Spirit He does impart,
Who now resides in our heart.
So we can know The God of Heaven,
and all the things He has freely given.

Which things we also speak,
Not in man's wisdom teach,
But we teach by The Holy Ghost,
Deep things of God we need the most.

But natural man does not receive,
He does not in The Spirit believe.
He is foolish in His mind,
He does not realize He is blind.

In The Spirit we can see,
Others may say how can this be?
But we have the mind of the Lord,
According to His Holy Word.

February 2, 2015

This Life I Have Deep Inside

My pencil on the paper moves,
As my spirit in me seeks,
Some deep down hidden truth,
My heart some secret treasure keeps.

The Word of the Lord came to me,
Through my hearing into my heart.
That Word sown was Holy seed,
Of God's own Spirit He did impart.

"You must believe" is what He said,
"Everything else is in your head
If you're going to talk the talk
You must also walk the walk".

I just want to praise The Lord,
Birthed in my heart by His Holy Word,
Is a song that I must sing
My God to me is everything.

This life I have deep inside,
Is a place I can abide.
There with Him We two are one
As it is with Father and Son.

So it is with Him and me
We'll live together eternally.
New life here has begun,
Ours the victory He has won.

In His strength I will go on
His Glories I will see
In The Spirit We are one
In His Victory He will keep.

My rest is blessed my sleep is sound
Angels watching all around
The thief defeated cannot steal
In Jesus Name I am healed.

I will sing and praise The Lord
He has come and settled the score.
By His Cross He has won
Now to God I am a son.

Something about The Blood and The Name
Into this world Jesus came
By His Blood He delivered me
Now in His Name I am free.

Where He leads me I now go.
And if I miss I always know
He is always here with me.
He turns all things good when I believe.

February 4, 2015.

"You Will Have No 'Word' If You Can See No Good."

Look for the good not for the bad.
First you must love, learn to be glad.
God always has the answer for you
When others ask, He always comes through.

When people come to ask you to pray
Lay on your hands begin to say:
"All of the good that you can see
You'll quickly find, it's not you but Me."

I love My children; to Me they look great.
You'll see it too, just learn to wait.
I'll open your eyes then you'll behold,
The beauty within will start to unfold.

I want to speak life to their hearts.
You'll be My mouth but you have to start.
And when you do then you will find,
You're moving in faith and speaking My mind.

Wonderful words and beauty unfolds
When they hear what's never been told.
Healing will come where hearts are broken,
Miracles too by what is spoken.

So lay on your hands and begin to speak.
Then from inside you'll pull from the deep.
My heart for My people out of your spirit,
Where We commune and they will hear it.

It will ring true and they will be blessed
When by faith you learn to rest.
Obey what I say We've much to do.
Now take this Word and follow through.

<u>February 5, 2015</u>

How Does That Work?

It's time to write what I do not know.
If I obey there will be a flow.
God never lacks for something to say.
Begin to write, get a Word today.

I don't know how God to others speaks.
But to me these last few weeks,
He talks when I write every time.
He gives me the meat while I find the rhyme.

The rhyme is on the surface don't you see?
It's what's in between that is so neat.
If you read with your spirit, you will find
Jesus is gentle, Jesus is kind.

He will talk to you and make it real plain.
He'll tell you the truth but you'll feel no pain.
He is able to cut into the heart deeply.
It feels so good when He does it so sweetly.

When the weight of the world falls to the ground,
Sometimes we don't know how it holds us down.
Then by the Spirit we can walk
With a spring in our step it's not just talk.

How does that work? You might ask.
My pencil on paper puts God to the task.
Our faith demands when we obey,
When we believe we have what we say.

God knows exactly what He wants to do.
He'll have His way if you follow through.
Do what He says when He says it.
Then you'll be moving in the Spirit.

He talks in your heart when you pray.
If you will listen He will say
Just what He wants you to know.
Sometimes He talks when you're on the go.

Sooner or later you'll have to do
Just what He told you to.
The sooner the better to act in faith
Time goes by when we hesitate.

Opportunities are lost when we're too slow.
Begin to act as soon as you know.
"I want to see," you might say
God would not be pleased, that's not faith.

The risk is too great for some to take.
But to disobey God would be a mistake.
Don't be afraid, be of good cheer.
Obeying God is an adventure.

Be excited for the opportunity
When God directs you will soon see.
The reward is great nothing compares.
Obeying God is like flying through the air.

It's exhilarating and peaceful too.
Soon very soon you will prove
There is nothing better than following God.
And complete your task as you travel this sod.

<u>February 6, 2015</u>

A Song and Dance Will Not Do

Write My Words as they come.
I will give them one by one.
My thoughts are too high for you.
Just a Word for you will do.

When by My Spirit I speak
You will get just a peak
Into the realm where I rule
It is there you'll go to school.

For in My Kingdom all is well
And I will help you to excel
In the things of the Spirit
If you will only hear it.

To satisfy your mind
You want to hear the whole line.
But by faith you will receive
One Word at a time when you believe.

So your actions must be timely
If just one Word, you regard highly
Then you'll get the truest flow
And secret things you will know.

Here is one thing for you now
By My Spirit I'll show you how
To press in where I am
You can do it I know you can.

It's not hard or complicated
Tell the truth simply stated
I won't hear all the stuff
Religious prayers I've heard enough.

I am The Truth, The Life, The way.
You must tell the truth every day.
Regard it highly as the means
Of gaining entrance to be seen.

It is there that I can start
To tell you things of the heart.
Words of Healing Words of Life
Healing wounds mending strife.

A song and dance will not do.
Until the truth I get from you
It is not that I don't know
I am not interested in a show.

Truth alone is the key
If you want to talk with Me.
Now I've told you how to do it
Tell the truth deep in your spirit.

Fresh and clean you will be
As you learn to follow Me
Be a Preacher of the truth
Then My people will follow you.

I will take you to the place
Where every kindred every race
All who I call are My own
That I will gather around My throne.

All of Heaven will be there
When I meet you in the air
The time the season is at hand
So be attentive to My plan.

The Words I give you now proclaim
I'll use them in the latter rain.
They will go forth as I intended
With what I do they will be blended.

For I work all things together
For the good now and forever
It all fits into My plan
It all comes by My hand.

Go to now do as I say
Not tomorrow start today
There are hearts that I must capture
And bring them in to My pasture.

One more thing as you go
You will need to always know
It is by faith not by sight
You'll find My way when you write.

<u>February 9, 2015</u>

Concerning A Vision

Heaven opened the host peered down
To see me laying on the ground.
Looking up where I could see
All those looking down at me.

They seemed a bit amazed at me
And I somehow could past them see
The Mercy Seat and The Blood
On either side those great winged creatures stood.

I somehow know that God is calling
Come up higher no more stalling.
Holiness I've prepared for you.
Behold My Glory and Power too.

It is no secret you know the way
Faith in The Blood, do it today.
You enter in and enjoy the freedom
Come in closer get what you're seeing.

Faith in The Blood will Holiness bring.
There you will get My full anointing.
It will rest on you wherever you go.
Others will see and they will know.

You are different than before.
God has opened for you a door.
Step through that door don't be afraid
There is God's plan for you He's made.

To get there you must let go
You are resting on what you know.
Take the leap and you will see
It is exciting to follow Me.

February 10, 2015

When You Lift Up a Shout

The only thing I know for sure
Is Christ and Him crucified.
Complicated schemes to men allure
But the key is that He died.

"Boldness with confidence" says He
Easy enough for you to say Lord
"Not if you have died with Me"
I guess that is what the cross is for.

Take up your cross and follow Me.
From pride and ego, I'll set you free.
Without reserve you will speak.
You'll cry aloud from the mountain peak.

Preach My Word loud and clear.
Preach My Word do not fear.
Preach My Word I am near.
Preach My Word for all to hear.

It is not complicated
You must be dedicated
To lift your voice lift it high
Foundations shake here is why.

When you lift up a shout
The devil you will route.
He doesn't take you seriously
When you're only whispering

The people are held in his grip
Tightly in their seats they sit
When with your voice you are demanding
You will soon see them standing.

Stomping Satan underfoot
More than ever will they look
More intently to the sky
For My return draweth nigh.

My people are still slumbering
They must stop their grumbling
Wake them up and you will see
A Church that has the Victory.

February 11, 2015
The Lord Will Keep the Feet of His Saints

[2] 1Sam. 2:9

You can't go back and undo what's done.
But the victory for you has been won.
Trusting in Jesus is what you will find
The only thing that brings peace of mind.

You've gone too far you'll never get back
The devil keeps nagging a persistent attack.
All things are possible when you believe.
God's Almighty Power you will receive.

The Lord shall keep the feet of His saints.
The wicked shall be silent in the night.
In his own strength the saint will faint
But his God takes up the fight.

The Blood of Jesus is on our side.
Right there in your heart it is applied.
Now His Spirit from deep within
Gives you the power the fight to win.

Jesus beat Satan once and for all.
We get the victory when we call
In The Name of Jesus, on The Lord.
We overcome by The Blood and The Word.

So by faith we move the mountain.
Devils tremble when we start shouting.
In Jesus Name they must flee.
Jesus has given the victory.

I once was dead now I'm alive.
The devil thought he had me, I revived.
Jesus has a plan just for me.
He went to the cross to set me free.

Now this has become my testimony.
Jesus set me free for eternity.
Satan thought he had me he was wrong.
Now forever I'll sing Jesus song.

Jesus will do anything for you.
He will begin when you tell the truth.
It may seem hard when you start.
You must trust Him with all of your heart.

He will very tenderly
Stand you up on your feet.
He will then keep you free.
He simply says follow Me.

There is no end to this Psalm,
It goes on your whole life long.
Living in Jesus every day
He is The Truth, The Life, and The Way.

<u>February 16, 2015</u>

Leave This World a Better Place

God in the beginning made
A man and to him power gave.
Over all the earth you shall rule,
But Satan played him for a fool.

Follow me the serpent said.
He did not mention you'll be dead.
Adam and Eve surrendered that day.
Their power and dominion was taken away.

Satan became the God of this world.
Then at man his darts he hurled.
For thousands of years he had his way.
Then Jesus came to put him away.

They should not have killed The Lamb of God.
For when they pulled Him beneath the sod,
Only a short time did they celebrate.
Then Jesus arose and destroyed the place.

All power is given unto me.
I send you out with authority.
In this world you will reign
When you pray in Jesus name.

"Take dominion" God did say,
Then man quickly gave it away.
Jesus came and got it back
He sends us forth with no lack.

He gave us power at Pentecost
So we could preach and teach the lost.
We are His salt to save the world
If the salt doesn't work it will be spoiled.

So with new birth the blessings come
And with them responsibility to run.
Run the race and win the prize
Wasting time and gifts is not wise.

And when the race is finally done
You a crown of life have won.
You'll be one who ran his race
And left this world a better place.

February 23, 2015

To My Father Gladly I Ran
3 (Based on The Lord's Prayer)

We press into the realm of The Spirit
By faith not sight we just do it.
Healing comes when we confess
By His wounds we're healed, there we rest.

Sure enough the pain goes away
We learned by faith we have what we say.
In God's Kingdom of the Spirit He rules.
How to come for healing He has schooled.

Jesus taught us to say when we pray:
"Thine is The Kingdom the Power and The Glory."
And to The Kingdom we go everyday
But now listen to the rest of the story.

By The power of My Blood
And in the authority of My Name
Before My throne you have stood
And there you proclaimed.

By Your wounds I am healed
And so you were filled.
By My Spirit with healing
And that strong healthy feeling.

I Am The Way The Truth and The Life.
I hold the answer to all struggle and strife.
When you're sick by faith My Kingdom comes.
To you brings healing My will is done.

The Kingdom the Power The glory are Mine.
By faith My Kingdom comes time after time.
The Power the Glory come the same way.
You must believe when you say:

"Thy Kingdom has come
Thy will is done
Your Power is all over me
And with my eyes your Glory I see."

By faith you will see
You have what you say.
Now you must believe
What I taught you to pray.

My Power and Glory don't happen by chance
By faith in My Word you must take a stand.
Lift up your voice and boldly proclaim
My Power and Glory in Jesus Name.

All of the plans I have for you
Will come at last when this you do.
So listen to your heart now it is thrilled
My Kingdom My Power My Glory will fill.

On earth just as My people have prayed
As it is in Heaven is what they have said.
My will be done the victory won
My Kingdom Power and Glory have come.

You who have learned to move by faith
Will bring it to pass when you say:
"Your Kingdom, Power, and Glory Lord
Have come to us now, by your Word."

Heavenly scenes now unfold
Of The Power and Glory as foretold
By those who in The Spirit see
My Kingdom My Power and My Glory.

To you with eyes to see
And ears to hear
Will you now believe
To The Lord draw near?

Or shall I for another look
For someone to believe My book
Don't hesitate I will not wait
Do it now or you'll be too late.

Selah.

Who now will lift their voice and proclaim
Thy Kingdom has come in Jesus name.
Thy will be done in earth right now
By The Power in The Blood that's how.

My Kingdom and Power and Glory
Fully manifest now you see.
My Power and Glory all over you
My Realm of the Spirit is here too.

Lift up your voice loud and clear
Do you believe My Kingdom is here?
With My Spirit comes My Power
I show Myself strong this very hour.

Shouting running lifting up hands
To My Father gladly I ran.
My Father in Heaven Your Kingdom has come
And here in the earth Your will is done.

February 24, 2015

What Is It That You Do?

What is it that men do
That requires no God?
Do they fear their own doom,
When they're placed in the sod?

Death is the end of existence they say.
The life they choose is to live they're own way.
I'll be my own judge I don't answer to you,
But death surely comes then they can't choose.

The Spirit they say doesn't exist
But theirs quickly falls into the abyss
Where cries of torment ring in their ears
No hope of escape no end to the years.

No, no, no, that won't happen to me
That stuff doesn't exist don't you see?
When I die I'll just go away.
There's no reason you see to be afraid.

One thing for sure dead men don't move.
They have no control over what others do.
Wills and legalities are only options.
You won't even know if they took your directions.

You no longer choose falling you lose.
Others now decide what happens to you.
Your body in the grave,
Your spirit unsaved.

Oh that's right you don't believe in the spirit.
When you were alive you wouldn't hear it.
There is only one way for you to be saved.
You must believe when you call on His name.

Jesus is calling He is The Way
But you would not come you would not pray.
Now it's too late your life here is done.
Eternity now for you has begun.

Jesus saves! That is good news.
Jesus is Lord, now let Him choose.
Be born again a new life to live.
New life forever to you He will give.

What is it you do that requires no God?
In just a short time you'll lay in the sod.
I pray this poem will get you awake.
Call on The Lord Jesus before it's too late.

<u>February 25, 2015</u>

The Last Call Is Sounding Now!

Without works faith is dead
But too often we work instead.
Of believing when we pray
Acting like we have what we say.

Are you secure in what you can do?
Or do you trust The Lord to come through?
You can't be lazy do your part
But to believe is where you start.

Prove Me now says The Lord.
Trust Me to keep My Word.
When old age has come to you
You will know I'll see you through.

When your day comes you will see
That you've done well to trust in me.
Cares and worries are not your lot
Peace and joy are what you've got.

Others will follow you
Your Blessing will Bless them too.
Do not falter do not bend
I'll be with you to the end.

Of this age it's almost done
My Church the victory almost won.
The call goes out just once more
For I'm about to close the door.

Be sure to love in these last days.
There are so many that don't know My ways.
With My Church all love will leave.
With only hatred men will grieve.

The last call is sounding now.
Some will hear it from your mouth.
Come in closer you will see
My Kingdom, My Power, and My Glory.

February 26, 2015

You've Been Slow in The Past

You hold the keys to My Kingdom.
They unlock the truth when you use them.
It's up to you not up to Me.
My Spirit I've given if you please.

So walk by faith not by sight.
It is now time choose what's right.
The first step must be taken
If you want to step the second.

When you can't see
You must trust Me.
You'll find My Power
This very hour.

Thoughts may come
To distract
But victory is won
When you don't look back.

As you follow you will see,
In The Spirit more clearly.
Eyes to see is what you get
Ears to hear and better yet.

Understanding of things I've said
While others sleep in their beds.
You My knowledge will behold
And My wisdom will unfold.

Things unseen by the world
Are plainly written in My Word.
You will have eyes to see
Faith is the way to follow Me.

You must believe that you will hear
What can only be heard with spirit ears.
Commit your way to hear and see
Move in faith and follow Me.

When you're alone you must write
Out of your pencil what isn't sight.
Will come into view and you will see
Only by faith can you follow me.

You've been slow in the past
But if you write at long last
A Word will come from within
It will be like a river flowin'.

February 28, 2015

Out of My Heart

We don't have a very nice house
Material is worn on the arm of the couch.
It's stained a little too, as the dog lays there
Guarding the door intruders beware.

In their little bed lay two more
The one that sheds laying on the floor.
Seven grandchildren coming and going
Kinda' messy inside outside it's snowing.

The carpet is worn on the floor
The dogs have clawed the back door
When the dogs are gone I'll fix it up
Every time one goes we get another pup.

People coming and going all the time
Smiling laughing that's a good sign.
Always dry and warm in here
In summer we cool it down with an air conditioner.

Sometimes we hurt sometimes we heal
Sometimes we hide the way we feel.
Kids and grandkids keep coming and going
I guess inside they have a yearning,

To come back home and visit awhile
Most of the time they leave with a smile.
Just wanted to stop and say hello
What's that you're drinking can I have one to go?

It's just love and comfort weathered and aged
A pretty good drink when the storms rage.
It will all work out it always does.
God always keeps us in His love.

The older I get the more I see
There aren't many left older than me.
Some things are no more a big deal
Now eternity seems to be more real.

We don't have a very nice house
But caskets are nice and neat.
It really doesn't matter about the couch
Soon I will bow at Jesus feet.

I searched the records at Polk Home
To find my older brother who died alone.
I told the lady there that Dad didn't say
Anything about Robert who died that day.

Before I was born long, long ago
Severe brain damage IQ zero.
Just a vegetable but still alive
Pneumonia finally took him at age five.

I wonder if I'll know him when I get there
Or if in all the wonder I'll even care.
I know in this life we work to eat.
But looking over there seems to entreat.

Now a lifetime of plowing and sowing seed
The crops are coming in I have to feed
All who are hungry and want to know
Everything God gave me before I go.

Write! Write! Write! He said to me.
What? What? What? I couldn't see.
Now every time I say OK Lord
Out of my heart comes another Word.

There may be just one who is blessed
To read this poem that I have left.
But that one is worthy of my time.
That must be the one God had on His mind

When He sowed the seed and watered it too
All the time He was thinking of you.
And now so that you would not miss it
He gave it in rhyme to me by His Spirit.

March 2, 2015

I Won't Sit Here While Life Goes By
[4] (Based on 1 Cor. 14:1 and [5] John 7:37,38.)

Rivers don't stop they continue to flow.
Sometimes they run fast sometimes slow.
If it was but a lake it might run dry
But rivers it seems have an endless supply.

Out of your belly if you believe
Rivers will flow with relative ease.
You don't have to pump it or make it go
You just open your mouth and let it flow.

To follow love how could we miss?
And also we're told desire spiritual gifts
But rather that ye prophesy
And here if you will be the reason why.

Your words go ahead of you today
You have now what you said yesterday.
Love and gifts come from The Giver
Out of your belly they'll flow like a river.

Prophesy is what you can do
You will speak His plan for you.
If instead of a river you have but a dribble
Then of His plan you'll have very little.

To prophesy is to act in faith.
When you start you don't know what you'll say.
There is a risk in what you don't know
But you have to start to get a flow.

Your sons and daughters shall prophesy.
That is God's Word and He doesn't lie.
Everyone is a daughter or a son
His eye is on you your time is come.

Will you now obey His Word?
Will you now let Him be Lord?
Then open your mouth open it wide
He plainly said you would prophesy.

Hold your tongue if you fear
What those will think who gather here.
What God thinks of you is the reason why
You should obey Him and prophesy.

Untold blessings of gifts and love
Will come to us from God above
Or we could leave bored and dry
If you choose not to prophesy.

Rivers start with just one drop
If just one Word is all you've got.
Give it now and be ready
More Words will come they'll be steady.

He said if you believe you'll get a river
He should know because He's the Giver.
But how will I look if nothing comes out?
Then lift up your voice and give a shout.

No matter what men do or say
I for my God will move in faith.
If I fall on my face He'll give me the grace
To get up again and run this race.

I won't sit here while life goes by
I'll get up and prophesy.
There are rivers of blessing in me
And with my voice I'll set them free.

The Words will go out like water flow
And wash over the people from head to toe
God will touch them. The reason why?
Because in obedience I prophesied.

March 4, 2015

Human History

Human History begins with God.
He made man from the sod.
Everything else is His design.
He even created time.

By faith they looked for Him,
Who created everything.
They found His way is the best.
Follow Him you will be blessed.

But then there entered iniquity,
From where is still a mystery.
A beautiful angel became a snake,
They listened to him, they made a mistake.

In his pride man thought he knew,
Better than God what he should do.
He reaped the reward of his wrong.
Now his life is a sad, sad song.

God took him back anyway,
Is willing to forget his yesterday,
But there remains in the man,
A need to be god if he can,

Somehow do away with Him,
Who created everything,
He says the creation created itself.
Nothing created everything, from nothing sells.

Everyone buys it happily,
Now from God they can be free.
I'll be my own god, and do things right,
What's right and wrong in my own sight.

To rule his own life did not work,
Left to himself he got worse and worse.
Finally, in his desperate state,
He cried to God, but too late.

To undo the damage that he'd done,
So many lives already gone,
God took him back anyway.
He's willing to forget his yesterday.

But somehow within the man,
A need to be god if he can,
Somehow do away with Him,
Who created everything.

March 9, 2015

Your Life Has Only Been Lent
[6](From Jonah Ch. 2)

All of the things of this life will pass
And the only thing left at long last
Will be that that is of the spirit realm.
If you sow to the spirit, you'll do well.

For a crop there waits for you
Because you attended to what is true
You didn't waste time with lying vanities.
You set your heart the Lord to please.

Take time to praise Him from your heart
Don't wait till later now's the time to start.
Eternity is forever you know
Everything here is going to go.

Don't clutter your life with frivolity
Flies in the ointment don't you see?
You have a mission, you're God sent
Your life here has only been lent

To this earthly realm for a season.
Heaven's purpose is the reason.
To rescue souls that wander here
And birth them from over there.

Citizens of Heaven they become
When you another soul have won.
Then their remaining time on earth
Will be to tell others of the new birth.

So don't let this life swallow you
As Jonah was you will be too.
If you observe lying vanities
They'll pull you down to the grave.

No matter how far you've gone down
You're not stuck you don't have to drown.
Lying vanities forsake them now
It's not hard this is how:

Praise The Lord all of your days!
Praise Him now in every way.
Walk by faith not by sight.
What you see will take to flight.

Find something to be thankful for
Thank Him for it you'll think of more.
Soon you'll see you have been blessed
Keep on praising you'll get the rest.

Of all the blessing He planned for you
It's up to you to follow through.
Heaven will open God is pleased
When you stop observing lying vanities.

What you can see touch taste smell or hear
Will soon be gone don't hold them dear.
Only the spirit will at last
Be all that's left of your past.

March 18, 2015

Some Are Red, Some Are Blue

Life is like an ocean,
Upon which I drift along.
Until a storm comes up again
I sing a happy song.

Dark clouds on the horizon
Tell of trouble yet to come
For me another opportunity
To trust God for the victory

There are seasons and there are times
Valleys deep and mountains to climb
My God keeps me through it all
Even when I forget to call.

He has kept me all these years
Through times of joy and times of tears.
One thing I can always say
God's been faithful all my days.

Some I've helped along the way,
Others help me from day to day.
It all works together for my good,
Though at times I've not understood.

What was happening when it happened,
I couldn't see my heart was saddened.
But then in time it became clear
The Lord was always very near.

Leading, guiding, showing the way
He brought me through the toughest days.
When the waves grow tall, I can rest
And know in God I am always blessed.

I have no particular place
That I am going in this race.
In this life, I'm just passing through
I am part of God's pit crew.

Others running toward their goal
Sometimes they run into a hole.
Blow a tire or run out of gas
To run their race, they will not last.

With my tools I repair
Take them from a world of care.
Fill them up and send them out
With God's Word and a shout.

Some are red, some are blue
Some a little worn, some brand new.
They come from every walk and place
And go out again to run the race.

I have not many followers
Those I've helped follow others.
They run to goals that they see
Those goals have little to do with me.

To know I've helped them along the way
Gives me courage for each day.
For another may limp in
To my tools I'll go again.

I'll give them Mark, Luke, and John
Before long they'll be gone.
To run their race, the prize to win
But me and my tools will be waiting.

For another and another
There is always a sister or a brother.
From the race they wander in
With my tools I work again.

Some may say I'm not leading
I guess not I'm too busy feeding.
For a crowd I have no time
When one's life is on the line.

March 19, 2015
I See You Lord, And That's Enough

All knowing God to you I pray,
You're everywhere and here today.
Your Power too and your Glory,
How I love to tell the story.

How you created everything,
Starting with absolutely nothing.
You simply spoke and it began,
You didn't have to lift a hand.

To think that I can talk to you,
I only need to tell the truth.
When in Jesus name I come,
Your attention I have won.

These precious thoughts, too big for me,
I see only through a glass dimly.
I do my best in faith to pray,
And you've been faithful every day.

So it is with heavy heart,
All my burdens I impart.
To your cross where they belong,
And I know it won't be long.

Until I see the victory,
In all the things you've done for me.
But in my heart there is a song,
Praising you Lord all day long.

A song that I can always sing,
And I know that it will bring,
Peace to me that makes me say,
Thank you Lord for today.

No matter what the world does,
I can always know your love.
When with my heart I look up,
I see You Lord, and that's enough.

March 20, 2015

Just Another Day, But Yet

Gray is the day and wet,
Just another day but yet,
Something's not the same,
He brought a knowing when He came.

His Spirit settled on me,
His anointing I received.
Now The Gospel is the seed,
To the hungry I must feed.

It the broken heart will heal,
And to the captive it reveals.
He has come to set you free,
He lights the way don't you see?

Crushed and bruised you may be,
He brings to you, liberty.
This is your time don't delay,
The Savior comes to you today.
[7] Luke 4:18

March 26, 2015

I'll Love Him Too, In Jesus Name

Though all forsake You Lord,
Not me, that's my word.
Peter promised with a vow.
He didn't know he was proud.

He doomed himself with his pride,
His hour came he did hide.
With his denial he lost face,
Jesus restored him by His grace.

If in haste you bow your back,
You may find that you lack.
The thing you said you'll never do,
Has never ceased to follow you.

When it bites you from behind,
You will see you were blind.
Hatred is a harsh judgment,
To the Lord it is repugnant.

When what I hate that I do,
For me there is no excuse.
O wretched man that I am,
Call on God's Sacrificial Lamb.

His Blood will wash away my sin,
And I'll learn to love like Him.
The vilest sinner He came to save.
That was me, I'll do the same.

Not to judge the sickest soul,
For him My Lord hung on a pole.
As for me, His loves the same.
I'll love him too in Jesus name.

March 27, 2015

Because You Dared To Follow Me

One by One they will come,
Into the promise I have won.
Things you've heard of the past
Have come to you at long last.

Many are excited for the season,
But you are for another reason.
All your labor for The Lord,
And now you'll see your reward.

They will preach, they will teach,
To the desperate they will reach,
With The Gospel loud and clear.
To everyone that will hear.

As they answer to the call,
I'll hold them up, they will not fall.
Signs and wonders, I will do.
And their gifts will come through.

Those who come will be healed,
And with My Spirit, they'll be filled.
They'll return and bring their friend,
And I will bless all of them.

So it begins with just a few,
But there is no end to what I'll do.
If on Me you will wait,
I will open the flood gate.

On those who come I will move.
When they go out I will prove.
What they got was for real.
My house again will have zeal.

My Spirit cannot be contained,
It will break out in latter rain.
As this rain keeps falling down,
It will soak into dry ground.

Life will spring from desert floors,
That life that is forevermore.
A blooming desert you will see,
Because you dared to follow me.

April 4, 2015

If In My Plan You Want A Part

"Light out" at the top of the tablet,
A note I made so I wouldn't forget,
To get a new bulb and turn it on,
Then all the darkness will be gone.

Ironic the light shines on the cross,
To go out on Good Friday, troubling loss.
I made a quick note, I was troubled to see,
The rest of the page was talking to me.

Praying and writing work together,
What's deep in your heart is recorded forever.
There were my notes from Friday A.M.
But I want to preach on the resurrection.

"They won't hear though I rose from the dead".
They've not believed the prophets or Moses, He said.
Judgment is no longer politically correct.
Warm and fuzzy is all they ever get.

"Light out" at the top is what I writ,
But the next line God so true, I know it.
Communing with God I began to scroll,
What He said to me "no passion for souls".

Not me God, I don't want to hear it,
But on the inside I know it's His Spirit.
Talking to me and now I have written,
On the next line "no zeal for Heaven".

But God you know we're happy down here.
You've blessed really good, we're full of cheer.
Healing, money, friends, as we travel this sod,
But then He said " no fear of God".

"The eminent peril of those out and about,
Is of little concern, when your light is out."
Good News, The Gospel will awaken your spirit.
But only for those who are desperate to hear it.

To Me belongeth vengeance, I will repay,
For their foot shall slide on that day.
Their end is at hand, no time to waste,
What comes their way, comes with haste. (Deut.32:35)

I saved you, you did not deserve it.
I put in your heart My very own Spirit.
Hell had marked you for its own.
Without Me, you were alone.

From the bowels of the earth the flames leap,
Just beneath the sinner's feet,
Waiting for that last gasp of breath,
Then to be swallowed up by death.

Forever lost, don't you see,
This is your day of opportunity,
To warn the wicked of his way,
He's fast approaching Judgment day.
[8] (Ez.3:18)
Now share Moses, [9] Deuteronomy 32:35,
If their spirit, you want to revive.
On Ezekiel 3:18 make a stand,
Or the blood of the sinner I'll require of your hand.

Let My Word pierce your heart,
If in My plan you want a part.
I've got Good News for your spirit,
If you are desperate to hear it.

April 7, 2015

So Lord, My God, And My Friend

If I could write a poem for You,
Of all the wonderful things You do,
I suppose it would never end,
For You continue each day to be my friend.

Blessing me from day to day,
Every hour along the way.
When I lay down to sleep at night,
You're there to say "all will be right".

Though I don't know the way to go,
You're there each day the way to show.
What the future holds I do not see,
But whatever it is, there you will be.

Others come with complications,
Looking for my directions.
If I can get them connected to You,
I know You will bring them through.

Faith it seems is all I know,
But some are looking for a show.
Power is good if they know what to do,
When the show is over, the moment of truth,

Will come when they alone must stand,
And back down the devil with their command.
God's Word in their heart when they shout,
Will shake the devil, and cast him out.

So Lord my God, and my Friend
This poem from my heart to You I send,
And for those whom you send to me,
I'll keep sending them on to Thee.

April 9, 2015

Just One Voice

If I could sing a song for You,
I'd sing and to my heart be true.
For there is where You talk to me,
And give me sight so I can see.

I cannot imagine what it would be,
To be empty inside, unable to see.
Left alone with my thought and reason,
Would make my life a very dry season.

Dried up with no life at all,
Only a moving, breathing shell.
Always looking for life in a thrill,
But fleeting emotions could never fill,

The void inside at the end of the day.
When I'm all alone and have something to say,
But no one to hear or talk to me,
That for me would be terribly lonely.

For You Lord who know me best,
Are there each night when I take my rest.
Comfort I find when I lay my head down.
For the last thing I hear is the sound,

Of Your voice bringing comfort to me,
Lifting my burdens giving me peace.
Though no mountain I climbed, or valley low,
Your Word I had the privilege to sow.

While others to lofty heights aspire,
If I can be just one voice in the choir
There I will happy be,
Knowing You're inside of me.

Ordering my steps and leading the way,
Moved by Your Spirit every day.
I've no desire for another's crown.
The right one for me to have found,

Will be the reward I'm looking for.
It may be plain, to others a bore,
But when I cast it down at Your feet,
I'll know that my life has been complete.

Nothing lacking or left undone,
Because in the Spirit we are one.
To follow my heart, is to follow You.
So to my heart I will be true.

And know that peace at the end of the day,
Comes to me when I hear You say,
Trust Me now and take your rest,
While you sleep I'll do what's best.

I love the preacher and the singer,
But to me you've given the pleasure,
Of writing psalms in a rhyme.
I seem to do it all the time.

So thank You Lord for the gift,
May these lyrics give a lift,
To just one, or two, or three.
Lift them up, help them see.

That the gift He's given You,
Is in your heart, to it be true,
And fulfillment you will find,
You'll end the day with peace of mind.

April 10, 2015

I Want You to Live Innocently

God formed Adam out of the ground,
When He looked about no mate He found.
He took a rib from Adam and made Eve,
Just for you Adam, to your wife you shall cleave.

Adam was made in the image of God,
God made Adam from the sod.
When He took Adam's rib he wasn't complete,
He put him back together when He gave him Eve.

In His own image, God made man.
Then He took a rib out and put it back again.
His image now is the man and his wife.
The two are how God started life.

Be fruitful, multiply, fill this place.
You are the beginning of the human race.
Subdue, have dominion over fish and fowl,
Take charge of everything, you'll learn how.

I want you to live innocently,
From every tree in the garden you can eat.
From the tree of the knowledge of good and evil,
Do not eat, it your innocence will kill.

God took pleasure in the man and his wife,
They walked and talked and enjoyed life.
They had good fellowship in the cool of the day,
Never any guilt, never any shame.

God hasn't changed how He feels about man,
Still loves to fellowship when He can.
But guilt and shame get in the way.
They make it hard to hear what God has to say.

By the virgin Mary God had a Son,
She called Him Jesus, He is The One.
Who takes all the sin, the guilt, the shame,
So we can fellowship with God in Jesus name.

It was for His good pleasure, He made you,
By the Cross of Christ, He made all things new.
You can walk and talk with God if you're saved,
If you're not, just call on Jesus name.

April 11, 2015

I Was Just A Kid In Those Days

"I'm gonna be a preacher", is what I said,
I don't know how that got in my head.
"What you gonna be when you grow up?"
Somehow that's just what came out.

I remember Oral Roberts in a tent on TV.
I remember how we wondered if it could be,
That God was really moving among men,
And not just far away, up in Heaven.

I was just a kid in those days,
Doing kid things, finding my way,
Didn't seem very long till I had a wife,
Standing at the altar, I knew it was for life.

We should go to Church now, we're grown up.
But I couldn't play the game, this is serious stuff.
Get in or get out, God seemed to say.
So we decided to get in, all the way.

Then we bought a house, the neighbors were saved,
The pressure was on, for us to do the same.
We're good Church people what are you talking about?
It would be a couple years, till we found out.

Praying, reading, seeking The Lord,
I finally gave up, and got reborn.
Went to a big meeting, they were talking in tongues.
Whatever they have, that is what I want.

April 23, 2015

This Open Door Will Soon Close

Though the horizon we always view,
We can forever toward it move,
And never get there though we try,
Just over there where land meets sky.

If we ponder just a bit,
We are now standing on it.
For where we looked to yesterday,
Is now where we are today.

While we yearn for goals unmet,
We miss what we have for what we can get.
Savor the gift of today,
Before all your days have gone away.

A grateful heart,
is where to start,
If you are headin',
In the right direction.

When you the gift appreciate,
You will find it's not too late,
To lift up your eyes and behold,
The road for you as you grow old.

Many there are that yearn to know,
What you from Me can to them show.
They are moving toward their horizon,
They need from Me all you can give them.

A mighty army there must be,
To bring in the harvest, you will see.
Now is the time, it's not too late,
You will see don't hesitate.

This open door will soon close.
Will another open? No one knows.
You will die if you sit,
It's time to move, get on with it.

April 24, 2015

What Is True Is What Endures

The days come and go,
They may bring a tale of woe,
But whether news is good or bad,
Of this one thing I can be glad.

Jesus is always here with me.
He forever faithful will be.
He's proved His love every day,
When He came, He came to stay.

Though the cares of life obscure,
What is true is what endures.
The same Jesus who brought me in,
Has kept me daily close to Him.

So as I travel on,
Through this life, not on my own,
But with Jesus every day,
He is here to lead the way.

April 27, 2015

But Wait God

I don't know about anyone else,
I can only speak for myself.
All of my religion was in my head,
Until that day I was raised from the dead.

You can't come out of the grave and not know it,
Everything you do will show it.
There's been a change come over you.
You're not your old self, something's new.

Your heart and your mouth are connected,
What's really in your heart will be reflected,
By what you say when things aren't right.
Jesus yoke is easy, His burden light.

The world tends to beat people down,
On the inside they wear a frown.
From your heart you release a word,
To see them smile is your reward.

You bring light and life wherever you go,
Those you greet seem to know,
That there's more going on than what they see,
And maybe there is cause for them to believe.

A little spark can light a fire,
Sometimes those flames leap higher and higher,
Until inside they can no longer contain,
They yield to God and get born-again.

That's what happened to me long ago,
Now I sow The Word wherever I go.
Just a little spark in someone's heart,
May be enough to give them a start.

I don't aim to set the world on fire,
But if in you I can create a desire,
For more of the wisdom of the Lord,
Maybe you'll consider reading His Word.

Fear of God is the beginning of wisdom.
Sometimes people fear what they been missin'
If you knew what I'm trying to say,
You may do better on judgment day.

That seed will root and start to grow,
You won't be satisfied until you know,
What only God can impart,
Deep inside a brand new heart.

So if you're still reading these lines,
Give up your religion, you know it's time.
To know for sure down inside,
You must be born-again to be satisfied.

Then you can rest in what Jesus did,
You are complete, in Him you are hid.
Whatever He did, you did it to,
"Well done My Son", God loves you.

But wait God, I didn't do anything!
That's exactly why God had to bring,
Everything you need to receive,
Christ crucified, you must believe.

You must now stop your trying,
Believe it's done, you won't be lying.
With your talk you must start,
Your mouth is connected to your heart.

Thank You Lord Jesus, now I see,
You've already done everything for me,
I'm born-again by You alone,
Now I feel like I just came home.

April 28, 2015

Jesus Is The Standard

If you are breathing, you are proud.
Did I say that out loud?
It is the nature of the beast,
A sad deception to say the least.

The thought was planted long ago,
When Eve thought "I can be as God".
Every human born since then,
Is born with pride, born in sin.

Pride was found in Lucifer,
Now it is bred in our character.
We can't help it; we're born that way.
We must deal with it every day.

Remember Jesus is the standard,
Compared to Him, we are measured.
All of us come up short,
No matter how hard we work.

We always need a Savior,
If with God, we look for favor.
He will not accept anything less,
Than Jesus who gave His very best.

So in Jesus we can hide,
And still live when God comes by.
As He hid Moses in the rock,
So in The Spirit we must walk.

If in Christ, I am crucified,
Then in Christ, I am made alive.
So it is never, about me,
Only in Jesus, I am free.

When The Spirit leads the way,
He'll speak of Jesus; He will not stray.
When Jesus is lifted high,
He'll draw all others to His side.

It's never about what I have done.
But always how Jesus won,
Over me in my prideful ways,
To set my feet on The Rock to stay.

So I have nothing to brag about.
If not for Jesus, I'd be left out.
I'd still be dead in my sins.
But thanks to Jesus, I'm born-again.

So to you I now say,
Look to Jesus every day.
He's the standard by which you're measured,
Thank God in Him, you are hid.

May 4, 2015

With The Blood I Agree

Jesus has become The Standard,
By which all men are measured.
There is not a man,
Who can before Him stand.

No matter what I see,
When I look at you and me,
I'm sorry to report,
We always come up short.

No need to feel so bad,
This Good News will make you glad.
God has chosen us in Him,
He has hidden us within,

Jesus His only begotten Son,
With Him now we are one.
So as I look around,
All I've ever found,

Is lovely people everywhere,
For me to judge would not be fair,
For God has hidden me in Him.
I will not look on another's sin.

Without Him, a filthy rag,
Is all I have, no need to brag.
God has chosen us in Him.
Not because we do not sin.

We have no good that we can bring,
God has given us freely everything.
For His good pleasure we are free,
With us in His Son He is well pleased.

I am not any better than you,
I'm hidden in Christ, you are too.
If I see you thru God's eyes,
I cannot then criticize.

That would undo The Cross,
Jesus suffering would be lost.
The Blood cries out "you are free".
With The Blood, I agree.

If I take that Grace from you,
I will take it from me too.
I will follow Jesus lead,
By example help your need.

May 5, 2015

One Way

Every attempt of man to appease
Is evidence that he is not pleased
With Christ Crucified God's only way
Was, will be, and is today.

Jesus said I am The Way, Truth, and Life,
But man in his pride continues to strive,
To please God by some other means.
Pride just seems to be in his genes.

"Give me religion, I'll earn my way"
But all of our "earning" by the end of the day,
Cannot please God even one little bit.
It's time for the church to get over it.

God's love for you is freely given.
All blessings are yours, including heaven.
Christ is The Way, He wasn't lying.
It saddens Him to see you keep trying.

What's the matter with them, don't they believe?
My love came by the cross; they refuse to receive.
No gain from religion, they should expect.
When The Gift of My Son, they continue to reject.

May 13, 2015

You Can't Fake It

I have two cars and a truck
For most people that would be enough
But a motorcycle is mine as well
I got a lot of stuff you can tell.

A big house and a garage too
Four dogs seems like a zoo.
Bought a shed for the overflow
I've got everything don't you know.

You would think I'm very blessed
I didn't know "Hot or Cold" was the test.
You've been weighed in the balance and found wanting
Not Hot nor Cold but lukewarm is a bad thing.

Not rich but poor concerning judgment
Blind you've been to His commandment.
In the spirit don't look now you are naked
God knows everything you can't fake it.

Forget the stuff get with God
Before you go beneath the sod.
Change your thinking, be restored
You must get Hot for The Lord.

May 14, 2015

Appointed to This Very Hour

[10] Heb. 12:2 "-Who for the joy that was set before Him, endured the cross-"

I held the whip and then the rod
I pressed the thorns onto my God.
I drove the nails into His hands
No thought I had to loose His bands.

Still He loved me to the end.
I caused His death He calls me friend.
He would be right to burn my soul
But life for me was His goal.

When to the cross He set His way
He could see another day.
When grace and love would abound
Where His Blood once ran down.

He gave His all held nothing back.
His love for me has no lack.
How could I hold onto anything?
All to Him I gladly bring.

All of me to Him I owe.
My life I give for Him to sow.
I take up my cross and follow Him.
By my death others will win.

That may sound sad
But He's made me glad.
The life I gave
Doomed for the grave.

The cross I took
Has another look.
On the other side
Eagle's wings I ride.

Silver and Gold
I may not hold
But in my hand
Is God's plan.

Life and light and liberty,
Touching, healing setting men free.
I died to that old earthy life
To fly like an eagle above the strife.

Every care I have lost
It was nailed to His cross.
No more work for me just rest
He carries me through every test.

All He promised I now receive
My part is only to believe.
He lives in me in my heart
And still desires to impart.

Life and light and liberty
Touching, healing setting men free.
Now He does it by my hand
I'm so glad He worked His plan.

He sowed His life as a seed
Bore fruit enough for every need.
Who by our sin caused His death
Now follow Him into our rest.

And rise again endued with power
Appointed to this very hour.
To touch and heal and set men free
With life and light and liberty.

<u>May 19, 2015</u>

Do What He Says

Sometimes I search within my heart,
Looking for God to impart,
Some light or wisdom for me today,
But if He's talking, I don't hear Him say,

Anything about the stuff,
That's all around, more than enough,
To make you wonder what's happening?
But He isn't saying anything.

So I pick up my pencil and start to write,
And sure enough His words become sight.
As they begin to appear,
His Spirit draws near.

"I've got you covered,
My Spirit hovers,
over you
in all that you do.

You may not see it at the time,
But I'm gathering in all that are mine.
You are part of the plan, don't stop now,
Stay in the flow, you'll soon see how,

It all works out to My Glory,
When at last all will see,
My Glorious Church in this hour,
Full of My Spirit, full of My Power."

Sometimes I feel like I'm losing ground.
Then out of my pencil comes the sound,
Of The Lord's voice loud and clear,
He lets me know, He's always near.

Obedience to Spirit is required,
If we expect to be inspired.
Our yieldedness is what avails,
If we want The Lord to prevail.

The Lord to me said to write,
He talks to you too, you can turn on The Light,
By doing what He said inside.
When you do, get ready for a ride.

He will take you to heights unknown.
You will find you're never alone
He is always faithful and true.
Do what He says, He'll use even you.

Prime the pump with the Word you know.
Soon like a river, the words will flow,
Watering the desert that's all around,
Bringing Life to all the dry ground.

This is the time that He will use,
All that are His, it's time to choose.
Will I be lukewarm, and come to naught?
Or get red hot and be used a lot.

Do it now speak it out,
Lift up your voice, begin to shout.
If you don't know what to say,
Speak in tongues, do it today.

As you speak begin to believe,
That God is in it, you will receive,
The induement of Power, He told you about,
It comes from the Spirit, when you shout.

When Jesus cried, with a loud voice,
Lazareth came forth, everyone rejoiced,
Death and darkness yield to command,
With your word you take a stand.

Don't be timid, that is to doubt,
Say it plain with a shout,
Let the saints be joyful, tell the story,
Sing aloud give God Glory.

With the high praises of God in our mouth,
Higher still when we praise with a shout,
A two edged sword He puts in our hand,
To fight the battle, take back the land.

Now I've sharpened my pencil twice,
I'm running out of time and rhyme.
As this psalm comes to a close,
God has spoken, His will made known.

May 21, 2015

No Lofty Perch

Sometimes I get really full,
His Word and Spirit on me pull,
As I draw near,
It becomes clear,

His love for me,
I can see,
His plan,
Is in hand.

As The Scripture he unfolds,
For me a future He holds,
Not with Me in the lead,
But in the stampede,

I will find Him at work with wrenches,
He calls me to join Him in the trenches,
No lofty perch,
From which to lurk,

But in the muck and the mire,
With the one He desires.
"There My power resides,
Thrust your hand in My side,

Not faithless but believing,
You will be receiving,
That enduement of power,
The very hour,

You reach out,
Begin to shout,
The victories in hand,
When you make your stand,

On My Word is The Rock,
Where the thief you will stop."

<u>May 25, 2015</u>

Your Need Is Great

The way up is down
You will hear the sound
Of His voice very clear
When you learn to draw near.

Humble yourself is the way
Without Him you are nothing today.
Yesterday's manna won't do
Today we start out brand new.

In life we fight to stand
We take our place as a man.
But this life has an end
And at last we will bend.

But while we still live
We have time to give
Our life to another
To Jesus our Brother.

In our heart He will give
His Holy Spirit to live
Now we are one
To God we're a son.

God gives Grace to the humble
Our pride will cause us to stumble.
Put our knees to the ground
The way up is down.

The miracle goes to the need
Humble yourself and concede,
Your need is great
Before it's too late.

Have pity on me Lord
According to Your Word
Give me power to preach
So more souls I can reach.

<u>May 27, 2015</u>

Love of The Father

My children will always have a home
While I live they will never be alone.
With wings of eagles they fly away
But they're welcome home anytime, any day.

June 1, 2015

Move On

God only knows what the future holds
We have the words the Prophets foretold
Concerning The Church some things are clear
But individuals too I hold dear.

Perils it seems are all around
Gators and snakes seem to abound.
Dealing with problems makes one weary
Constant struggle you don't see clearly.

God has given the overview
The details are up to you.
You can stay back and fight the devil
Or move on to a higher level.

June 3, 2015

We Can Keep It

All of the stuff
That gets on us
Can be washed away

But we can keep it
If we want it
And don't take time to pray.

People and what they do
Will gain control of you
If their burdens on you stay.

Give them to Jesus
This is what pleases
God will lift your cares today.

June 8, 2015

This Is What I Pray for You

The world it seems goes round and round
And never seems to stop.
Though my feet are on the ground
God calls me aside to talk.

I close the door behind me
The world I no longer see.
It's here that I get lost
In The Glory of His Cross.

Sometimes the answer comes to me
Sometimes the victory I see.
It is not the end I came to find
But the means brings peace of mind.

To be with Him and know He's near
Brings me peace and makes it clear.
To trust in Him is all I need
For He has promised to keep my feet.

As I go I have no fear
I can bring the world some cheer.
Not because I am so smart
But with God my day did start.

Glorious goals don't come to me
But a few souls I oversee.
There I labor for the Lord
Just helping one is great reward.

More of God is all I seek
To know Him more every week.
He writes on the table of my heart
He talks to me about my part.

He helps me see and understand
He has many at His command.
We're all different in some way
We must be careful when we pray.

His plan may differ for me and you
To your heart you must be true.
Only in Christ can you be free
I dare not infringe on that liberty.

My prayer is that my life's story
Would be one that gives Him glory.
This is what I pray for you
That your life brings Him glory too.

<u>June 15, 2015</u>

The Cross

The cross now empty stands
Was made by human hands.
God gave a living tree
Now it marks eternity.

What was once alive
We caused it to die.
A cross we made of it
And used it for a little bit.

It only took one day
God's Son on it to slay.
Now it forever marks
The way to God's heart.

The Gift He gave back then
Calls to the heart of men.
When we see that old wood cross
We can't help but count the cost.

God dearly for us paid
With the wicked He made His grave.
A sinner's death He died
When Him we crucified.

How Jesus loved
He came from above
To us down below
This now we know.

He died so we could live
So now we live to give
This message of the cross
To those who are still lost.

Though the message has been told
It never will grow old
I'm still reminded of the cost
Each time I see that old wood cross.

<u>June 16, 2015</u>

The Bottom Rung

Lord your voice I need not hear
But to know that you are near.
Brings me peace and gives me rest
Yet I yearn for your best.

For you to write on my heart today
Satisfies in a different way.
A personal touch from You to me
Somehow makes me feel complete.

This is life to me
A great sense of security.
I know I'm loved because I've heard
From You to me a personal word.

More than cool water on a hot dry day
Just one word to hear You say.
Hunger for food I have not known
Like the hunger for You that has grown.

In my spirit where loud and clear
Is the cry for more of your voice to hear.
My daily Bread I so need
So I open my Bible and begin to read.

What You have already said
Can by me be easily read.
I begin to underline
What to me comes alive.

Sometimes just a spark ignites
A flaming fire burning bright.
A Candle shining in the dark
The Light of Your Word in my heart.

Just one Word can volumes speak
I may ponder it for weeks,
Until my life has been marked
By Your Word in my heart.

This is the cycle I've come to know
Your Light and Truth in me grow,
With a blessing occasionally
When I share it with one in need.

I am so often caught off guard
To hear from one whose life's been hard.
When out of my spirit I begin to speak
A thought that came spontaneously.

After I ponder what I've said
I know it's from The Word I read.
This Living Word how can it be
That You would use the likes of me.

Selah

I spend my life on the bottom rung
Helping others to catch on.
And as they begin to climb
I turn around and there behind

Is another floating in the sea
And as they float over close to me
I pull them up with Your Word
Until they know in their heart they've heard.

You speaking, leading, showing the way
When I begin to hear them say,
God talks to me in my heart
Then I know they'll do their part.

Up Your ladder they begin to climb
And as they do I look behind
There floating on the sea
Is another floating close to me.

Selah

That's all for now, waiting for me
A window to fix so people can see.
What's outside without the crack
From their view it will not distract.

Perhaps outside their window will be
Another floating on the sea.
With a Word they can help them catch on
But will they live on the bottom rung.

Or will they climb to the top
Of God's ladder until they stop.
At a place before they've passed
The last will be first and the first last.

When all our ambitions have been done
And all our songs have been sung,
When in His Spirit we all are one
I'll have spent my life on the bottom rung.

But please don't feel bad for me
The bottom rung is life to me
I pray you'll have eyes to see
On the bottom rung Jesus and me.

June 19, 2015

The Night Is Far Spent

Awake out of sleep
He seems to speak.
From far away
I can hear Him say:

The night is far spent
It is time to repent
Peace is not from sleep
But is found when His Word you keep.

Now is the time
To get things in line
To move at His Word
You know you heard.

<u>June 22, 2015</u>

Get Rid of the Cow

He is here right now
While we ponder how
We'll be totally free
When we can meet.

All the conditions we've set
Looking forward and yet
It doesn't seem to click
Like the carrot on the stick.

We always put off
Our faith being soft
But His Presence and Power
Are here this very hour.

Faith's time is now
But our sacred cow
Is what He'll do when
And we'll be blessed then.

It is always tomorrow
So much to my sorrow
We never believe
Right now we receive.

We've conditioned our thought
That tomorrow's our lot
Never today
Is what we always say.

So then the next day
Our hope is the same
That later we'll see
His Power to set free.

But it's never now
And yet some how
We don't seem to get
If God's not here yet.

Then He never will be
Because the same unbelief
That we have today
With us will stay.

But God is the same
He doesn't change
What He was yesterday
He will be today.

If He wasn't here, then
No need to ask when
Get rid of the cow
Faith's time is now.

Will you now believe
And thereby receive
There's no need to wait
Tomorrow's too late.

The time to receive
Is when you believe
He's here this very hour
In all of His Power.

Revival is coming they say
But Jesus says I'm here today
The "prophets" have spoken
Now only a token

Is what you will get
Because revival's not here yet.
What will it take
For us to awake?

Faith's time is now
Break the sacred cow.
If you want to break out
Then lift up a shout.

Lift up your voice,
Begin to rejoice.
Do not stop shouting
Till you're no longer doubting.

He is here all the time
We must get in line.
His Word will not change
We cannot stay the same.

What is gonna be
You will never see.
It is finished He said
Then He hung His head.

His dying Word I believe
And right now I receive.
His Life is in me
And now I can see

That revival has come.
It may start with just one
But I'm full of His Power
And this very hour.

Every weight every fetter
Is gone forever.
Revival's begun
For everyone.

Who dares to believe
And by faith will receive
All that He said
All His Blessings instead.

Of the junk you now carry
And will till you're buried.
If you don't now believe
That now you receive.

June 23, 2015

Out of The Blue

All around
Not a sound
Nor do I see
Who sees me.

The spirit world
Where I've been born
Is more real
Than what I feel.

There God is King
Over everything
We grow in spirit
And still don't hear it.

But a knowing
Keeps us going.
Things that are true.
Come out of the blue.

When we obey
That inward sway
We will find
Peace of mind.

June 24, 2015

There Is No End

Some will come
To the one
Who for them died
He was crucified.

And as He lives
So He gives
Life to all
Who on Him call.

He by His Spirit will
Yet beckon still
To all who yearn
And want to learn.

The deeper things
Of what life means
Of this world does not
Satisfy a lot.

Frustrations build
Life cannot fulfill
The deeper need
That we must heed.

And so our heart
Is to find our part
Of God's great plan
For every man.

To this end we look
Into His Holy Book
His treasures we receive
When we believe.

And His Spirit too
Within us moves
Blessings abound
Everywhere are found.

We savor these
And He is pleased
To have this communion
And with us be one.

I could go on
And on and on
There is no end
What a friend.

June 26, 2015

Many Mysteries

Write He said
So write I did
And now look
I've got a book.

Poems, quite a few
Not just one or two.
Prophetic Psalms for those
To whom my heart goes.

And some just for me
But many for everybody.
Hardly any have been read
They stay in a binder instead.

What next I don't know
But to The Lord I go
To inquire of The Lord
What to do with these words.

Lift them higher, don't you see
There the fire they will see
Like a candle in the dark
They bring light to the heart.

Give the gift I gave you
And not to just a few
Give the gift for all to see
The gift will draw men to Me.

Many mysteries of the heart
Enlightenment I will impart.
Peace to those who read
The psalm will fulfill their need.

To commune with My Spirit
I'll speak to them, they'll hear it.
As they learn to tune in
A walk with Me will begin.

Their life's purpose will unfold
They will no longer be so cold.
I'll warm the hearts with My Word
As they're moved by what they heard.

I have longed for My people
To worship Me and not a steeple
To walk with Me can only start
When you find Me in your heart

July 6, 2015

On Wings of Eagles
(can be sung)

Lord I give my heart and mind to Thee
Take these hands and feet and let them be.
Ever always in your service Lord
That I may live by your Holy Word.

Chorus: On wings of eagles I can fly
Above the clouds and touch the sky.
Bound to this earth I could not stay
With Jesus someday I will fly away.

Somehow into my heart Jesus you came
Since then I have not been the same.
Just one thing in life can satisfy
You in me and that's the reason why.

Each time I come I am looking for
More of You I find in Your Word.
Just one touch inside is all I need.
A touch from You will make me complete.

<u>July 7, 2015</u>

Show Me How

Set your heart to know
The truth that I will show.
You will have eyes to see
Let your heart follow me.

Ears to hear
Are very near
When you look
Into The Book.

On the hearts of those I love
I send a Word from above,
To open treasure for you to see
You must come on bended knee.

I resist the proud you know
Grace to the humble flows.
I will move on your heart
If you're ready to do your part.

Ready Lord? How can I be?
You must commit your way to Me.
I spoke to you in the past
Will you now obey Me at last?

Volumes I will open up to you
If you will to your heart be true.
For there is where I now live
All My wisdom ready to give.

Ears to hear and eyes to see
Reside in the heart of humility.
In the mirror you must start
Tell the truth from your heart.

I'm not looking for a song and dance
I can tell at just one glance.
Open your heart don't be afraid
I'll heal the wounds life has made.

Wholesome, healthy, innocent too
Is the heart I've prepared for you.
Others have your heart betrayed
I have come, with you to stay.

Give Me your heart, don't hold back
You will find you will not lack.
Seeing, hearing, loving too
You'll do those things that I would do.

By My Spirit, saith The Lord
I will fulfill My Holy Word.
You'll be My hands, My feet, My voice
All because you've made the choice.

To open your heart, all of it
That I may fill you with My Spirit.
With Light and Life and Liberty
Faith, Love, Joy you'll see

A peace that you have never known
For you have finally come home.
More secure you'll never be
Than when you give your heart to Me.

"How can I Lord? Show me how"
Tell the truth, tell it now.
Talk to Me as if I'm there
I'll lift from you all the care.

Talk to Me every day
Talk to Me the same way.
Honest, truthful, from your heart
I from you will never part.

You will marvel and wonder too
At all the things I will do.
Through you I will touch
Others who need so much

To hear from Me and know
That I really love them so.
Always humble you will be
You will know it's not you but Me.

A life worth living you will find
And you will have peace of mind.
You and I are as one
The life I intended, you have found.

July 13, 2015

God Never Changes

God never changes, He's always the same
Here all the time from the first day He came.
I get distracted and lose my way
God never changes, He's always the same.

July 15, 2015

Thank You Lord

Life it seems can overwhelming be
When everything's piling up on me.
Peace I know is down inside
But from me now seems to hide.

The kids are grown and grandkids too
Coming and going just passing through.
The house is needing a few repairs
Cars need fixed a world of care.

Sometimes I sit
For a bit
Then up I stand
And with my hands

I go to the task
Get things done at last.
When I think I'm almost done
I notice the list goes on and on.

Something's wrong with this picture
Life is gone for this fixer.
Never did get to the goal
I can't remember to save my soul.

What was my purpose anyway?
But to give God Glory every day.
Thank You Lord for helping me
Your purpose I served faithfully.

July 21, 2015

Through A Hole

The world around me spins
But there's another world within.
Sometimes I'm torn between the two
So much so that I know not what to do.

So I begin to write
What's inside comes to light.
I begin to hear the sound
Of the world slowing down.

What seemed to be a maze
Now appearing from the haze.
Is slowly becoming clear
As it continues drawing near.

I from a distance see
Everything surrounding me
As though from another's eye
Looking down from the sky.

As through this life I go
Things happen that I don't know.
But when I'm looking down at me
Flaming arrows, I can see.

Many darts miss their mark
They were doomed from the start.
If one hits me with its flame
I'm alerted by the pain.

By faith I must quickly deal
Remove the dart, begin to heal.
How did the dart get inside?
Through a hole I call pride.

God protects me everyday
But my pride gets in the way.
Fiery darts can find their mark
If I let pride in my heart.

I could never judge another
Not a sister or a brother.
I am carried totally
By Jesus and His Love for me.

From this world I can rest
Trust Him to help me do my best.
Lord I come on bended knees
Do with me Lord as you please.

None of me do I withhold
Not my silver or my gold.
Your life for me you freely gave
Please let me serve you all my days.

The world around me spins
But there's another world within.
One will soon go away
In the other I'll forever stay.

July 22, 2015

The Love of The Father

He who gave His Only Son
Would not withhold from even one.
Of us who in Him believe
Freely now His blessings receive.

Not like us He is true
Never will He forsake you.
Nor can any take you away
You are His forever to stay.

The Love of The Father came to me
Opened my eyes and let me see.
Earthly dads try as they may
Cannot compare to my Fathers ways.

My Father listens and talks to me
His love imparts security.
Only who's loved can love another
Love is to know The Love of the Father.

Will you now His Love receive?
You have only to believe.
That He gave His Only Son
Has He now your heart won?

<u>July 30, 2015</u>

And Then Some Day

Lost, lost, all is lost.
Frivolity has a terrible cost.
Frivolous things are light it seems
The time lost cannot be redeemed.

You were away
The world moved on.
The devil to pay
The anointing is gone.

The more I rest
The heavier it gets.
My hand to the plow
My time is not now.

The end of the row
Comes so slow.
My reward at the end,
Do it again.

To throw off the load
And take the wrong road
Only brings dread
Of what lies ahead.

Back home I came
To more of the same.
No light I see
In front of me.

But if one frown
I turn upside down
The smile I see
Is reward for me.

I'll keep on diggin'
For what I've been gettin'.
Today I will see
Someone who needs

The things that I've found
When I'm plowing the ground.
Here in God's garden
I have found pardon.

Now I have seed
To sow to the need.
The heart is God's ground
Where I have plowed.

His seed I will sow
He'll make it grow.
As He waters and tills
Men's hearts will be filled.

But my lot for now
Is back to the plow.
A strange comfort I find
Work is good for the mind.

And then some day
I'll fly away
To where I don't see
But with Jesus I will be.

<u>July 31, 2015</u>

The Curse Causeless

Proverbs 26:2 As the bird by wandering, as the swallow by flying, so the curse causeless shall not come.

The curse causeless shall not come
There is nothing new under the sun.
Our struggles come for reasons known
You'll find that reason is your own.

The root of a thing is under ground
When you dig deep it will be found.
It's not seen now but soon will be
The curse will drive us to our knees.

The Holy Ghost and The Word of God
Will help us dig beneath the sod.
It won't come by thought or reason
Mental gains are but for a season.

The Holy Ghost will point it out
When He does lift up a shout.
You must forgive and let go
Of bitterness you did not know.

From Gods law we will not escape.
Gravity works God made it that way.
Even babies don't float away
By gravity on the ground we stay.

It wasn't right what was done
Way back when we were young.
That wrong has lodged deep within
Caused a bitter root to begin.

Silently that root took hold
Out of sight and now we're old.
"Do not judge" now judges me
It's God's law, like gravity.

The curse causeless has not come
When the cause within I have found.
To the cross it will go,
No cause for the curse anymore.

August 3, 2015

Only Believe

I know if I start
I will have to complete.
I don't have to be smart,
Just follow my feet.

Where they go
I go too.
No thought of their own
They make me choose.

And so when I write
My pencil leads.
It draws from inside
To my heart heeds.

The storms of life come
To everyone.
And when they pass
You sit down at last.

You ponder what happened
Sometimes you're saddened.
A terrible cost
But all is not lost.

When wisdom we've gained
From the wind and the rain
It helps with the pain
From the dragon we've slain.

A strange new world
Far away from home
Darts at you are hurled
From sources unknown.

You can't go back
So you must go on
But you seem to lack
Your vision is gone.

So now you must trust
In what you can't see.
Hear Jesus words
Only believe.

<u>August 5, 2015</u>

I Guess Not

Shall I a poem write?
Will it work if I type?
There is inside my heart
Living water to impart.

Write He said
Can I type instead?

I guess not.

<u>August 5, 2015</u>

Take Your Rest

Sometimes empty is what I feel.
Sometimes depleted, but still.
A strange settling peace abides,
Nothing stirring inside.

Several irons in the fire
None of which I now desire.
They will come at the appointed time,
But for now peace is mine.

Take your rest
You've done your best.
Learn of Me
You will see.

Greater still
I will fill
All the earth
With My will.

August 7, 2015

I Am The Way

Faith is a strange commodity
Belief in something you cannot see.
A connection of sorts if you get it
To the unseen realm of the Spirit.

God started with nothing at all.
Everything in with His Word He called.
The unseen God gave us all that we see.
Now it remains for us to believe.

The material world from The Spirit came
When God by faith called everything by name.
He that is made now can't see
Who made Him demands he believe.

He searched inside, found DNA.
Looked in the sky a long, long way.
Man has exhausted his intellect.
Where it all came from he doesn't get.

Through desire he must separate
From what can be seen before it's too late.
If he seeks he will find
Only from spirit comes peace of mind.

His anxious soul can now rest
Finally satisfied in his quest.
To know how and why he is here
God made him for His good pleasure.

"Come to The Father", Jesus said.
I am The Way not your head.
You must believe is how it's done.
Come to The Father by way of His Son.

Faith in Jesus is the key.
He died for your sin, do you believe?
He rose again and is waiting for you.
Your faith is seen in what you do.

When you believe you will act.
What can't be seen to you is fact.
Others will notice and begin to say:
"What's up with you, what made you that way?"

Jesus has become real to me
He gave me faith now I believe.
The realm of the spirit is more real
Than what I see, hear, smell, taste, or feel.

God did something inside of me.
Now I believe in what I can't see.
Faith connects me to the unseen world.
Read all about it in God's Word.

<u>August 8, 2015</u>

Haroon and Maddie
Married Today

Two they come still so young,
God will join them into one.
Where they go they do not know.
Together they will make a home.

Something they've never done before.
They will struggle that's for sure.
Trials of life will make them strong.
From them come the Victory song.

It won't be long till they find
God is faithful all the time.
They can in Him find their rest,
He will help them be their best.

As they stand here at the start
They tenderly give their hearts.
To each other to hold dear
While others watch and hold back tears.

Adventure lies just outside the door.
You've never journeyed here before.
Hold on tight enjoy the ride.
You go from here side by side.

From the old and battle scarred
Knowing life can be hard.
Don't give up when things go wrong
At the end you'll have a song.

We were you once long ago.
What we were doing we did not know.
We had fun and trouble too.
God has always brought us through.

Your kids will take your place someday.
They will give their hearts away.
With joy and fear you'll shed tears.
You've lived a life of many years.

Your life together begins now.
Put your hand to the plow.
If you keep God first in everything
You'll always have a song to sing.

"Papa [Gary] Rutter"

<u>August 11, 2015</u>

To The Point

The Cross of Christ
Is the beginning of life.
Death was defeated
If you believe it.

Eternity awaits everyone.
Good News because of The Son.
He who believes is born anew.
Forever alive God is true.

<u>August 14, 2015</u>

Do It Now

When we were born
The clock began to tick.
It either goes too fast or
Sometimes slows down a bit.

From day to day
We find our way.
From week to week
Our schedules keep.

Months go on
Seasons change.
A year is gone,
We do it again.

We live as if it will never end.
Working, playing, and then,
Time runs out,
We look about.

Could it be
Time for me
is over now?
But somehow...

I didn't think it would be like this
Just a little time one more kiss.
What about all my stuff
It seemed like it was never enough.

If I had more time...
I'd like to go,
But there's a line
And I'm too slow.

There are things to see
And places to go.
More stuff for me
I did not know.

It would be today
I'd like to stay.
But now it is time
At the end of the line.

And so the world goes on
Life for many today is gone.
When God created all of it
He set the clock, it began to tick.

The clock
will stop.
Time at last
Will be past.

The world will end
And that my friend
Can be found in The Book
If you care to look.

What you always wanted to do
Do it now before you're through.
You don't have the rest of your life
Jesus is coming, maybe tonight.

August 18, 2015

The Prettiest Thing You've Ever Seen

How desperately my soul
Desires to be whole.
To be set at liberty
From all the stuff be free.

Stuff goes around in my head,
All the reasons why instead.
Of just one encouraging word,
If I only would have heard.

Light in the darkness shines,
Just one word at the right time.
Can all the difference make,
Speak that word for Jesus sake.

Living waters deep inside,
From the world seem to hide.
Rivers Jesus said would flow,
Open your mouth let them go.

For every word you have
There is someone who's sad.
But sad they will remain
If we don't speak in Jesus name.

Let rivers flow out from you.
Fill a brown desert with waters blue.
The prettiest thing you've ever seen
The desert floor coming up green.

Seed time and harvest, don't you know?
Sow a seed, watch it grow.
The miracle of life comes by love
From our Father up above.

I don't know what you need?
But if you'll give it as a seed.
30, 60, 100 will return
Do what He said, you have learned.

<u>August 24, 2015</u>

Moving On

There is so much I do not know.
Sometimes there is no clear way to go.
Peace it seems is a rare commodity,
When all my thoughts center on me.

God seems hard to find,
Troubles overwhelm my mind.
No answer to them I can see,
Just one way to go free.

Leave them on the altar lay,
Trust The Lord for today.
He alone can bare the load,
Meantime I've got seed to sow.

Love will always find a way
For peace to happen every day.
Touch another for The Lord,
You will find there's great reward.

Devils hacking at your back,
Will fall away if you don't slack.
Keep on going for The Lord,
Be a champion of His Word.

The time is now to run the race,
You're rounding third, keep up the pace.
So many souls don't have a clue.
Will they be saved? Depends on you.

Living, learning, moving on,
Soon your days will be gone.
Sooner still maybe today,
Jesus will catch His bride away.

Then our preaching days are done,
So for now we must run.
The time is short do you believe?
Will you now this word receive?

Set your heart on things above,
Not of the earth you must love.
Let your life in Christ be hid,
Now and forever you'll be glad you did.

August 26, 2015

That Sacred Desk

Each time I mount the pulpit
I depend upon His Spirit
To move upon my heart
And show me where to start.

Once I get going,
It just keeps on flowing
Until it abruptly ends
Then I say "let's stand".

Then after I conclude
I pray as I am moved.
Again that sacred desk
Has put me to the test.

My preaching skills may lack,
Sometimes they don't come back.
God's Word I did impart
As it was written on my heart.

To Him I must be true
No matter what others do.
I cannot entertain
Or be frivolous in Jesus name.

To me it's not a lectern
Or just a place to learn.
The pulpit is much higher
A place of Holy Fire.

Like flies in the oil,
To treat it lightly can spoil.
That meeting place with Him
Between the wings of The Cherubim.

The reason I live
Is His Word to give.
In this life only death
Could take me from that Sacred Desk.

August 27, 2015

If I Seem to Lack

If with this pencil lead
I write what's in my head,
The words I cannot find
They're just not in my mind.

Because I ain't too smart
I just write what's on my heart.
My heart is like a tablet,
God with His finger writes on it.

There is a longing deep inside
Where the real me seems to hide.
To know Him even more
Than I ever have before.

It's always a preoccupation
That holds my attention,
So if I seem distracted
Please don't think I've backslid.

You only get part of me
Unless The Lord with me you seek.
That is where I'm at
If I seem to lack.

What you're looking for
Then look for it from The Lord.
There we two can meet
Together at Jesus feet.

August 31, 2015

But for Now

Troublesome times on every side,
Soon no place to hide.
Could this be that awesome day
When He comes to catch us away?

It may be, or maybe not
That He'll come and we are caught,
Up to Heaven with Him there
To leave at last this world of care.

But for now I can but write
From my heart where there's light.
Even as the sky grows dark
He shines His light in my heart.

If just one word I have for you
To that word I will be true.
I'll do my best in faith to give it
To you from The Holy Spirit.

September 5, 2015

The War

Now on the paper my pencil writes
What is hidden comes to light.
The gift is His, He gave it to me
It comes by faith, what is not seen.

The gift has always been personal
Sometimes for others, sometimes for self.
For the Church they seem to flow
A voice of comfort for all to know.

But now I tremble at the thought
That the gift will come to naught.
If I lay my pencil down
Will the gift fall to the ground?

And yet in my head it's empty,
I have not anything to say.
There is a warring in my soul
So much injustice in the world.

People hating, lashing out
Hurting others as they shout.
With their words they kill,
Yet the killing does not heal.

All the pain they have inside
Just continues to reside.
In a heart filled with hate,
Now for love is it too late?

The thief has come to steal and kill
He'll destroy you at his will.
But Jesus came to give you life
Give you peace instead of strife.

The Truth you need to be free
Concerns yourself, not those you see.
The problem is between God and you
He only moves when there is truth.

Learn to listen to what they say
Agree quickly with your adversary.
It's not hard if you try
God will show you the reason why.

Then if the truth you embrace
You can begin to run the race.
You will quickly gain much ground
When the Truth you have found.

September 8, 2015

All Is Well

I may be made of clay.
Sometimes I go astray.
But God in His Infinite Wisdom
Caused me to be born-again.

He took from me a heart of stone,
Replaced it with one of His own.
Not the blood pump but the spirit.
He made it alive by living in it.

It is not by my intellect
Or because I'm physically fit,
But by His Spirit He talks to me
Deep inside, it's a mystery.

God in us the hope of glory
According to the Gospel Story.
But all the clatter of this life
Against the spirit causes strife.

To press into that inner place
And get the plan to run the race.
Each day is Holy unto our God
Let His praises flow from this sod.

Out from you rivers will flow
If you can get where you must go.
Into the spirit realm is the place
If you want to run the race.

It's deep inside where you can't see
There's a well down there in the deep.
It's dry on top but it will flow
Into the spirit you can go.

Pray in tongues mysteries,
Praise in tongues new songs to sing.
Lift that language lift it high
Into the spirit you will fly.

Above the earth its muck and mire
To a place that is much higher.
Prime that pump with tongues unknown
Your well within will begin to flow.

God will speak from deep inside
From your spirit where He resides.
You too will in concert flow
Rivers of living waters will go.

Out from you when you speak
Life goes out to meet the need
Of all who in the desert dwell
They'll hear and know that all is well.

September 10, 2015

Make Us Preachers

Sometimes The Light shines bright.
What we see we do not like
So we draw back into the shadow
And hope no one will know.

But He who knows everything
Says "What are you doing?"
The Truth won't change for you
Although you want it to.

Wrong is wrong, right is right
No matter how you try to hide.
When God's place you try to take
You are making a sad mistake.

Over and over men go down
Away from God into the ground.
Earthy dirty they become
They run away from The One

Who can save them from their woe
But to Him they refuse to go.
"I'll decide for me what's right"
"I will do what I like".

"You'll be as gods" the serpent said
And so they were, now their dead.
"You won't surly die",
Is still the devil's lie.

No fear of God in the land,
Preachers fear to take a stand.
"Don't take my stuff, don't put me in jail"
All the while we're going to hell.

It's still the same we never change
Nobody standing in Jesus name.
Oh we gladly preach to the choir
As we fall into the fire.

God won't change His Word for you
All your wisdom will not do.
The foolishness of preaching is God's way
You better get to it before it's too late.

Judge us Lord, send The Fire
Consume the chaff, lift us higher.
Out of the muck and miry clay
Judge us Lord, do it today.

Give us grace to change our ways
While we still have a few days
To Preach the Cross of Christ
Be a beacon of pure light.

In the world's darkest hour
Make us preachers by your power
That we might preach "Jesus Saves"
As quickly we approach the grave.

Though the time for some has past
Lest we preach with our last gasp.
Some poor soul may never hear
Lest we preach with Godly fear.

Because You loved them they killed You
The Apostles loved, they killed them too.
Men are falling into the fire
We keep on preaching to the choir.

Hell's a fire, don't you know?
And to that fire you will go!
But if a preacher you will hear
Your heart will change by Holy Fear.

September 12, 2015

The Unseen Trade

God gave Adam the freedom of choice
But Adam listened to the wrong voice.
The devil told Eve what to do
Eve told Adam and he did it too.

The devil gained control of Eve
Promised power but he deceived.
Eve used her power, told Adam to do
That very thing that God said not to.

From that day it's been a power play
What others do we want a say
To be our own god and even more
To be god over others we look for.

A taste of power is never enough.
We tend to want more and more of that stuff.
Our lust for power is never satisfied.
Craving for more believing a lie.

Pride pushes on an ego trip
As it takes, others must give.
Eve thought she got but really she gave
And so it is the unseen trade.

Not many mighty or noble are called
God has chosen the weak in the world.
He will confound the powers that be
The power of men will get no glory.

All of the fighting going on in the world
Fighting for power they want to be gods.
Such it has been for millenniums now
The power they crave their sacred cow.

The last shall be first the first shall be last
Soon all the struggle will be in the past.
The givers will be caught up by the Lord
The takers will get their just reward.

September 14, 2015

Hidden Treasure

Into a field for treasure I looked
That field is known as The Holy Book.
Hidden in its pages bound
There a treasure I have found.

The truth is what I sought to see
There it was staring back at me.
When I saw the treasure of God
It was Him looking at this vessel of sod.

'Twas He that gave so much for me
With joy He hung upon that tree.
To buy this vessel of earthen treasure
He purchased me for His good pleasure.

God who sees all the world
Searches for goodly pearls.
He paid dearly with His life
To buy the pearl of great price.

He used this poem for a net
Has gathered you among the rest.
For your soul He paid dearly.
Will you now His treasure be?

Angels now linger near
To gather His pearls and hold them dear.
Say yes to Jesus don't delay
For the rest will be cast away.

September 16, 2015

The Sower Soweth

I know not what a man might need
But if I can to his spirit feed
The Word of God tried and true
I know what that man will do.

He'll ponder what was said
Try to figure in his head.
But where he in this world will go
That Word will begin to show.

A candle you cannot hide.
To cover it will cause a fire.
That Light will dispel the doubt
Unless you put the candle out.

So this seed I will be sowing
As long as Jesus keeps me going.
All those seeds will someday sprout
Unless I put my candle out.

September 21, 2015

Prophets, Wise Men, and Scribes

Treasures here for you to find
Come from my heart, not my mind.
Where God has made His abode
New things and old from life's road.

I write them down as I was told
So that the reader can behold
The things that God wrote on my heart
Are written for you, that's my part.

I have been sent from Him to you
So with this poem I follow through.
Fill your heart with His Word
Guided steps are your reward.

Your spirit man will grow strong
You will see, it won't be long.
Begin to pray every day
If you know not what to say.

Pray in tongues from your heart
And to your heart He will impart,
Treasures you will find
And you'll have peace of mind.

The realm of The Spirit where God is
Is His Kingdom where He lives.
It co-exists at the same time
With this world of yours and mine.

All He promised comes to you
From The Spirit realm, they're true.
They're all there and they wait
For you to speak in Jesus name.

Very near, not far away
We must believe when we pray.
They listen now to what we say
For our words they must obey.

Life and death are in our words.
Life can be our reward.
Two steps forward and one back
That won't do, that's why we lack.

Our words reveal what's in our heart,
Be consistent from the start.
If you can bridle your tongue
You'll find your heart can be won.

For with the heart we must believe
And with the mouth we receive
What we say and don't doubt
You will see, it will work out.

God has sent to you a scribe
Out of my treasure to you I write,
Treasures new and some old
Now to you have been told.
[11] Matthew 13:51,52 & [12] 23:34

September 23, 2015

Yesterday's Manna

Time it seems is life's measure.
Long life we think is our pleasure.
A life span is given to everyone,
Short or long we've a race to run.

But time goes by relentlessly
It does not stop when we sleep.
Each day is closer to the end
Another day we did spend.

Where they went we don't know
The days just seem to come and go.
Before we can figure where they went
We find they've nearly all been spent.

And for what we might ask
As we toil at some task
Our reward for living today
Is another day to live the same way.

That same thing that we did before
Each day seems the same old chore.
Can't write the same poem over and over
Something new we must discover.

So to that Old Book that we read before
We read again and we know for sure
Something new that we've never seen
Is right there where we've already been.

So life in this world may vary
Our days may be boring or scary
But fresh manna from Heaven
Will make this life worth living.

New wine won't work in old skin
Yesterday's manna quit working
Time has moved on
The race is not done.

We cannot go back
We can't stop in our tracks.
The Spirit is always moving
If we're not, then we are losing.

Open our Bible today
Read it and then pray.
Listen to our heart
We'll know where to start.

Obey the voice of The Spirit.
He never told us to quit.
Do what He said don't wait,
Fresh manna's only fresh today.

<u>September 25, 2015</u>
Then Jesus Came

God created Adam perfectly
But then the mystery of iniquity.
Adam sinned
His life did end
And he passed his sin to his kin.

Things went down from there,
Only Noah and his family were spared.
When the great flood was over
Noah planted a vineyard
And the sinning started over again.

God made a promise to Abe
To him a son He gave.
But then came Jacob
A deceiver by nature
So the trend has been set in the clay.

Then Joseph was sold into Egypt.
There in that land he was equipped
To be a slave all his life
Till Moses brought light
Of God Who gave them a lift.

They came out of Egypt as slaves
God by His laws tried to change.
In the desert they did rot
Till their kids got their lot.
Great blessing and land God gave.

Through many Judges they went
They would rebel and then they repent.
Though good for a time
They then would backslide.
God then another Judge would send.

They cried to God for a king.
God heeded their cry but one thing,
The king made of clay,
Would sin the same way,
So their sinning and repenting remained.

Then Jesus came and did not sin.
God Himself would live within.
When anyone in Jesus believes
New life in Christ he receives.

No longer The Law over our head
To The Law the new man is dead.
When by The Spirit we are moved
We flow in God's Law of Love.

So the battle today
Is how much does the clay
Surrender to The One inside
Instead of his passion and pride.

We have the advantage of power,
The Name of Jesus is a strong tower.
We can yield to The Spirit He gave
By what He does we will be amazed.

September 29, 2015

It Is with You as Was Foretold

With stammering lips and another tongue
I've ordained that My song be sung.
You get stuck when you don't understand
But I've not come to take your hand.

Tis your heart I'm looking for,
You've worked so hard to keep it secure.
I'll take that stony heart from you
And give you one that to me is true.

In that new heart I will live
There you will gladly give
All of you to Me
You are now totally free.

Not a whit do you withhold
It is with you as was foretold.
You show forth praises from inside,
You're out of darkness in the light.

A peculiar people you've become.
You have believed in The Son.
No longer dry and taught of men,
You have a tender heart within.

Who now believes I Am inside
And will trust that I don't lie.
Will from your heart speak what's true
Your life will be the living proof.

That I mean just what I say
If from your heart you obey.
The wooing of The One within
You with Me in life will win.

October 2, 2015

Look for Good

You'll be as gods, the serpent said
As he tried to control her head.
And so the woman and the man
Played into the devil's hand.

And now born in every man
Is the desire to rule who he can.
We look at people every day
And think we know a better way.

But God is God, and we are not
To judge another is not our lot.
To love and give as we can
So many need a helping hand.

Until love opens another's heart
We've no word to impart.
As we listen we hear them say
Is there hope for me today?

Beautiful feet bring good news,
But their not pretty in combat boots.
Even the hardest heart will melt
When the touch of God he's felt.

When we judge we start a war
To their heart they shut the door.
Their sin they will readily admit,
If they can see their way out of it.

When we earn trust and not before
They will listen to our word.
What love started from without
Faith completes, wins over doubt.

So look for good if you're a teacher
Leave law and judgment to the preacher.
It works together for the good
When your part you've understood.

October 7, 2015

Great Reward

We should get in or get out
I said to my young wife.
Church is no place for doubt
So we began our new life.

We got in all the way
Up to our ears
The reward has been great
Over the years.

We've come a long way
From those early years.
God showed us the way
To overcome all our fears.

The sun is still shining
Though low in the sky.
There's no time for pining
Not even a sigh.

We're just rounding third
There's a play at the plate.
We've already heard
The Umpire call safe.

Our enemy's defeated
Jesus is Lord.
Many times it's repeated
In God's Holy Word.

Your race I can't run
But you can be sure
If to Jesus, you come
You'll find great reward.

October 8, 2015

This Is The Day

As I lift up my voice
Draw my lungs full of breath
And begin to rejoice
Drive away death.

Life rushes in
Filling the room
Where just had been
Filled with gloom.

God in His strength
Fills the place,
He remains at length
Brings a smile to my face.

Awake sleepy Church
He seems to say.
Rise up from your perch
This is the day.

When My people with wings
Like eagles will fly
My praises to sing
Mount up to the sky.

To places unknown
In the heavenlies
To you I will show
When you follow Me.

To every problem
The answer you'll see
You just need to get them
To follow Me.

I Am The Way
The Truth and The Life
No need to stay
In all of that strife.

Light is My burden
And easy My yoke
When you get My Word in
To your heart that I spoke.

In your heart you know
My Word is true
Speak it where you go
They'll follow you.

You're not alone when you go
And you speak My Word
In their hearts they will know
By My Spirit I'll confirm.

Lives will be changed
Smiles will appear
Where once they complained
Now of good cheer.

The Good News is good
To the heart of the lost
When on My Word they've stood
And realized the cost.

They too will go
And preach the Good News
Soon all will know
That My Word is true.

This is the end
When all shall see
My Son I will send
To bring you to Me.

October 9, 2015

Break The Mold

What if I write
With nothing to say
Will He give light
In a different way?

Will I from deep inside
Pull up some mystery?
Will He with His finger guide
And begin to talk to me?

Something I don't understand
Something not yet seen
Will it come by His hand
If in Him I believe?

Strangers know
Not where to go
But He will show
Us here below.

You must write
You must start
You will find
I'm in your heart.

Listen, listen you will see
Be as truthful as you can
If you answer honestly
You will hear what is My plan.

My people sleep
They don't hear
They must speak
Do not fear.

Your faith will go ahead of you
I have a Word prepared.
When you speak you'll find it true
My Word through you I've shared.

Your head may fight
To be in control
Your heart is right
When you speak be bold.

Pretty soon you will be
Whenever the need is there
Instantly used of Me
To show someone I care.

Break the mold
Throw it away
Don't be cold
Start a new day.

The time is now
Don't be late
I'll show you how
You must awake.

To move by faith
You must talk
I'll have My say
You'll walk the walk.

It is exciting
To be free
You'll be inviting
The lost to Me.

Your heart I now unlock
From sin I set you free
For you I went to the cross
Of Me you can now freely speak.

Fear thou not
Only believe
You have got
Just what you need.

October 16, 2015

Good News for Everyone

He is The God of endless supply
That is the reason why
The world could not contain
All that could be written in Jesus name.

We are born of God above
When that eternal Spirit of Love
Comes into our inner man
And we get born-again.

Born of God not of man
A new creature in the land
No more in the dark
That light sets us apart.

We now have ears to hear
And see what's always been near
God's ways no longer obscure
In us have been born.

It's not about the doctrines of men
It's about being born-again
Once dead we're now alive
We live in a whole new light.

We could not see in the dark
But through hearing He did impart
Faith when we believed
His Word we received.

Christ in us The Hope of Glory
Has now become our story
The new man inside
Is where God resides.

Matthew, Mark, Luke, and John
Tell not about what is gone
But rather what began
Now spreading through the land.

Signs wonders and miracles
Heal the sick cast out devils
Manifest sons of God
Going about on this sod.

Good News for everyone
Because God sent His Son
He is no longer mad at you
To The Cross of Christ, He is true.

October 19, 2015

First Frost

First frost
Leaves turning
For the lost
He is yearning.

The fields are white
The grain is falling
To the harvest
He is calling.

Listen, listen
You will hear
We're still missing
Who He holds dear.

October 26, 2015

Singing His Song

The inner man is born-again
The outer man grows old,
What's of the spirit is forever
What is left goes cold.

This life seems but preparation
For what eternity holds.
Here it is we find salvation
And can I be so bold?

As to remind you dear reader
That God "so loved the world"
He sent His Son to be our leader,
And while Satan's darts are hurled

We follow Jesus ever always
Our mission to complete.
We call others all our days
To join us at Jesus feet.

We may falter we may fail
But our life tells a tale.
Thou life's trials can be a struggle
Our faith holds beneath the veil.

Substance and evidence they see
When we're steadfast you and me.
No matter what we follow Jesus
Because we know this is what pleases.

God who gave us everything
Now to others new life brings.
Through our witness and His Word
In our hand He's put His sword.

The whole world to God belongs
Until everyone is singing His song.
We've got work and purpose too
To this end may we be true.

November 4, 2015

Dogs Bark

Dogs bark, Cats meow, Sinners sin
The Preacher said
It's just the way we've always been
Until we're dead.

There'll be no sinning in the grave
Until then we need to be saved.
Every day is one day closer
To the day this life is over.

Yet we think we have no need
For all that God stuff others believe.
But this could be that very day
When death comes to take us away.

Then those words I so dread
"Depart from Me" is what He said.
Not now Lord, not like this
Just one more day I won't miss.

I will change, you will see
A different man I will be.
Dogs bark, Cats meow, Sinners sin
I end up doing the same old thing.

Be ye perfect is what He said
But I'm far from it and I dread.
My case is hopeless, I cannot do
Even one commandment let alone two.

There are ten laws that He gave.
They speak clearly "you must be saved"
From your sin before it's too late
With your Judge you have a date.

Such great love He has for me
He sent Jesus to set me free.
On the cross He took my sin,
Took my death so I could live.

You must believe it to receive it
Be born-again in your spirit.
Alive to God you become
You with Him are now one.

Now by faith we must move on
From our new heart sing His song.
A new creature He has made us
For by His Cross He has saved us.

November 11, 2015

The Unseen

Open your mouth wide
And I will fill it.
So we set aside our pride
And speak from our spirit.

As the words come out
The vision becomes clear
We lift up a shout
For Him we do hear.

If with my pencil, I write
What I do not know becomes sight.
Faith moves by what is not seen
To please God, you must believe.

So to my tablet I go
To write what I don't know.
But one thing I have proven
He is The Faithful God of Heaven.

My people are pleasing to Me
When on My Word they believe.
You keep on teaching
Even do some preaching
And by writing you'll cause them to see.

Write the vision make it clear
I by My Spirit am near.
If My people believe
My Spirit receive
My plan for them they will hear.

You must believe as a child
Like stepping into a cloud.
Though you don't see
You're obeying Me.
I'll separate you from the crowd.

For many have a form of religion
But from My power they've hidden.
Not moved by My Spirit
They wouldn't hear It
Now to you I do My bidden.

If you obey you will see
What I have purposed to be.
You must move by faith
Before it's too late
Then your race you'll complete.

November 13, 2015

As a Child

We tend to do what we've always done
Just keep on dancing to the same old drum.
Another beat by us is not heard
Till we hear the beat of God's Word.

We tend to read and not believe,
We have no thought we might receive
Miracles like days of old,
Only stories we've been told.

Could it be God's Word is true?
Is there a miracle for you?
If you read and then decide
You will tend to let it ride.

As a child you must come
Before you read believe it's done.
What it says is what I have
I will read it and be glad.

To know the love that comes my way
In His Word I read today.
By His stripes I am healed
Makes no difference what I feel.

I expect what I don't see
God has promised it to me.
Jesus suffered in my place
I am healed by His grace.

Even though I don't understand
I now trust in His plan.
As a child I now believe
Abundant life I now receive.

Sin, sickness, and death He defeated
Now His victory is completed.
I am the reward that He sought
With His Blood I've been bought.

He found me beaten and left for dead
He gave His life for me instead.
A new song I will now sing
He deserves the reward of His suffering.

Thank you Jesus, I now receive
Your work is finished, I believe.
By your wounds I am healed
Your Word is truer than what I feel.

<u>November 17, 2015</u>

Prophesy

No thought of my own
Do I bring to this poem,
But deep inside
Where He resides
Where He has made His home.

A stirring, a yearning
It seems I'm ever learning.
He desires to move through me
To open things I don't now see.

Prophesy, son of man.
Prophesy, if you can.
There are things that I will do
When you let Me move through you.

Like a rushing mighty wind
O Breath of God breathe again.
These dry bones begin to move
Come together take on sinew.

As we stand and take on skin
We will start to live again.
Breathe on us O Breath of God
Call your Church up from the sod.

Exceeding Great Army stand
With His two edged sword in hand.
Heal the sick raise the dead
Miracles are the children's bread.

This is the day, this is the hour
All the earth will see My power.
Put in the scythe the fields are white
Soon the day will turn to night.

In My power you will move
All My weapons you will prove.
You're in the battle of the ages
The fury of the devil rages.

There are souls on every side
They are Mine now Prophesy.
You will win with My Sword
When you obey My Holy Word.

<u>November 19, 2015</u>

The Upper Room

Wait for Power to witness, He said.
We witness no Power instead.
All the world can see
Is just another philosophy.

The Power fell on Pentecost.
All their inhibition was lost.
They staggered into the street
A crowd gathered to hear them speak.

Pentecostals out of control,
Resulted in three thousand souls.
Wildfire had broken out
Made you want to lift up a shout.

We think we're much smarter now
"I can build the church I know how"
And with all the methods of man
We try as hard as we can.

Some succeed and some don't
For each one that does, ten won't.
But if all it is, is a show.
Then why do I bother to go.

Some The Power want to see,
They watch it like watching TV.
Instead of getting into the flow
They sit there in the shadow.

The Spirit comes like a breeze
He moves on all who believe.
All who enter this room
By The Power will move.

The upper room is a place of belief
When you enter you'll feel The Peace.
All who for Him wait there
Will soon come out of their chair.

Wouldn't that be out of order?
Yes, well no, maybe sorta'.
If everyone as they are will remain
Then church can always be the same.

December 1, 2015

His Message I Will Always Be

Never thought about being old.
Seems so often I feel cold.
Life went by really fast.
Now nearing the end at last.

I hope I didn't impose on you
I don't like telling others what to do.
God is ever always on my mind.
He tries to get me to be kind.

That doesn't always work for me.
My spirit's willing, my flesh is weak.
If I ever caused you to fall
You can blame me; it was my fault.

If by me, you were blessed
Give God Glory, I passed the test.
A faithful friend He has been
I know He'll love me to the end.

Laying yet ahead of me
Some ups and downs I can see.
He holds my hand through all of it
Never falters not one little bit.

I will always sing His song
If life is short or if it's long.
I must always sing His praise
With every breath all My days.

When I look upon the cross
I can't conceive the awful cost.
How far He went to rescue Me
His message I will always be.

He loves me more than I can know.
And if His Love in my life shows.
Then all the days He gives to me
His love will I more clearly see.

<u>December 4, 2015</u>

The Time at Hand

Winter is coming on
All the leaves are gone.
Each day seems a little colder
All now living a little older.

So the seasons mark the time
To some the past has been kind.
They may want life to go on
Time to sing one more song.

Others whom life has beat down
May be ready for the ground.
All sense of hope has worn away
They've no desire here to stay.

But regardless of our past
The end will come at long last.
All that's been then will end
Before our God we will stand.

Did we receive the Gift He gave?
His Son He sent us to save.
Are we a giver or a taker?
Are we ready to meet our maker?

If Heaven is so great
Why would we want to wait?
Unless some soul we've yet to tell
About Jesus, Heaven and Hell.

We don't have the rest of our life
Jesus is coming maybe tonight.
Then our preaching days are done
No more souls can be won.

If we focus on our end
We tend to miss the time at hand.
Be a giver not a taker
Then we'll be like our maker.

December 14, 2015

But for Grace

To the Well I come to draw
From its depths I thought I saw,
Some fleeting truth that passed by,
Could it be the reason why?

So many are tossed on every wave.
Some new truth they seem to crave.
Outside The Bible they continue to look,
They have little regard for The Holy Book.

So with their head they try to see
What belongs to the heart if they believe.
The Word God gave is true.
It will open up to you.

You must believe it before you read it.
He brings it alive by The Holy Spirit.
That Word will quicken in your heart.
To you His Truth He will impart.

Then The Lord reminded me
On your own you cannot believe.
Your faith was imparted by My Grace
Present your heart as a blank slate.

Humble yourself if you want to grow.
Give up the stuff you think you know.
Read My Word as it is pure and true.
Let it begin to modify you.

Absolute Truth you can know.
The opinion of men you must let go.
God has Power we don't understand.
He preserved His Word though it's written by a man.

There is a reason not to believe.
If it can be wrong, we can be deceived.
We may think we know better than God.
That's dangerous ground for us to trod.

Many have gone that way,
Further from God they continue to stray.
Because they have followers as they trek.
Better a millstone was tied around their neck.

We need Grace to believe.
We must be humble to receive.
Our ideas are sacred cows.
Give them up as we bow.

He made a donkey speak,
He used us though we're weak.
He wrote His Word with a pen,
Though it was held by mortal men.

When we think of all He's done for us
It's silly to think He doesn't have the stuff.
Trust Him now His Word receive
It's a miracle for all who believe.

December 22, 2015

A Blooming Flower Will Be Found

If I could write a poem for you
I'd fill it with love and comfort too.
But when my pencil on paper writes
What's in my heart comes to light.

Sometimes I sit with pencil still
Trusting to move at His will.
Then He with me begins a flow
Of the things He wants us to know.

Of all the stuff we fuss about
There's just One we can't do without.
To be one with The Father, Jesus taught
That is why we were Blood Bought.

God paid dearly to have and to hold
Sometimes we let our love grow cold.
Everything we could possibly need
He already has, no need to worry.

Start in the morning alone with Him
To you peace of mind He will give.
Through the day He'll prosper your way
From within His Spirit will say.

A kind word for you to give
From deep in your heart where He lives.
He'll touch others and heal them too
A powerful team Him and you.

He'll speak to you down inside
His love for you He will not hide.
He paid dearly, and at long last
The reward of His suffering will come to pass.

His love for you He will complete.
When another of like faith you meet.
While others strain to find the way
Just let Him love you every day.

A Blooming flower will be found,
Nothing but desert all around.
When in your heart you believe
And His Sweet Spirit you receive.

The End

Scripture References

¹ 4 And my speech and my preaching was not with enticing words of man's wisdom, but in demonstration of the Spirit and of power:5 That your faith should not stand in the wisdom of men, but in the power of God. 6 Howbeit we speak wisdom among them that are perfect: yet not the wisdom of this world, nor of the princes of this world, that come to nought:7 But we speak the wisdom of God in a mystery, even the hidden wisdom, which God ordained before the world unto our glory:8 Which none of the princes of this world knew: for had they known it, they would not have crucified the Lord of glory
(1 Corinthians 2:4-8 KJV)
² 9 He will keep the feet of his saints,
and the wicked shall be silent in darkness;
for by strength shall no man prevail
(1 Samuel 2:9 KJV)
³ 9 After this manner therefore pray ye, Our Father which art in heaven, Hallowed be thy name. 10 Thy kingdom come. Thy will be done in earth, as it is in heaven. 11 Give us this day our daily bread. 12 And forgive us our debts, as we forgive our debtors. 13 And lead us not into temptation, but deliver us from evil: For thine is the kingdom, and the power, and the glory, for ever. Amen
(Matthew 6:9-13 KJV)
⁴ 1 Follow after charity, and desire spiritual gifts, but rather that ye may prophesy
(1 Corinthians 14:1 KJV)

5 37 In the last day, that great day of the feast, Jesus stood and cried, saying, if any man thirst, let him come unto me, and drink. 38 He that believeth on me, as the scripture hath said, out of his belly shall flow rivers of living water
(John 7:37-38 KJV)
6 1 Then Jonah prayed unto the Lord his God out of the fish's belly, 2 And said,
I cried by reason of mine affliction unto the Lord, and he heard me;
out of the belly of hell cried I, and thou heardest my voice.
3 For thou hadst cast me into the deep, in the midst of the seas;
and the floods compassed me about:
all thy billows and thy waves passed over me.
4 Then I said, I am cast out of thy sight;
yet I will look again toward thy holy temple.
5 The waters compassed me about, even to the soul: the depth closed me round about,
the weeds were wrapped about my head.
6 I went down to the bottoms of the mountains;
the earth with her bars was about me for ever:
yet hast thou brought up my life from corruption, O Lord my God.
7 When my soul fainted within me I remembered the Lord:
and my prayer came in unto thee, into thine holy temple.
8 They that observe lying vanities forsake their own mercy.
9 But I will sacrifice unto thee with the voice of thanksgiving;

I will pay that that I have vowed.
Salvation is of the Lord.
10 And the Lord spake unto the fish, and it vomited
out Jonah upon the dry land
(Jonah 2:1-10 KJV)

[7] 18 The Spirit of the Lord is upon me, because he hath
anointed me to preach the gospel to the poor; he hath
sent me to heal the brokenhearted, to preach
deliverance to the captives, and recovering of sight to
the blind, to set at liberty them that are bruised
(Luke 4:18 KJV)

[8] 18 When I say unto the wicked, Thou shalt surely die;
and thou givest him not warning, nor speakest to warn
the wicked from his wicked way, to save his life; the
same wicked man shall die in his iniquity; but his
blood will I require at thine hand
(Ezekiel 3:18 KJV)

[9] 35 To me belongeth vengeance, and recompence;
their foot shall slide in due time:
for the day of their calamity is at hand,
and the things that shall come upon them make haste
(Deuteronomy 32:35 KJV)

[10] 2 Looking unto Jesus the author and finisher of our
faith; who for the joy that was set before him endured
the cross, despising the shame, and is set down at the
right hand of the throne of God
(Hebrews 12:2 KJV)

[11] 51 Jesus saith unto them, Have ye understood all
these things? They say unto him, Yea, Lord. 52 Then
said he unto them, Therefore every scribe which is
instructed unto the kingdom of heaven is like unto a
man that is an householder, which bringeth forth out
of his treasure things new and old
(Matthew 13:51-52 KJV)

[12] 34 Wherefore, behold, I send unto you prophets, and wise men, and scribes: and some of them ye shall kill and crucify; and some of them shall ye scourge in your synagogues, and persecute them from city to city (Matthew 23:34 KJV)

www.ingramcontent.com/pod-product-compliance
Lightning Source LLC
Chambersburg PA
CBHW022105040426
42451CB00007B/130